KINGDOM OF THE UNJUST

KINGDOM OF THE UNJUST

BEHIND THE U.S.–SAUDI CONNECTION

MEDEA BENJAMIN

OR Books

New York · London

© 2016 Medea Benjamin

Published for the book trade by OR Books in partnership with Counterpoint Press.
Distributed to the trade by Publishers Group West

All rights information: rights@orbooks.com

First printing 2016

Cataloging-in-Publication data is available from the Library of Congress.
A catalog record for this book is available from the British Library.

ISBN 978-1-94486-902-1

Text design by Under|Over. Typeset by AarkMany Media, Chennai, India.

10 9 8 7 6 5 4 3 2 1

TABLE OF CONTENTS

Credit: Norman Einstein

INTRODUCTION

Through the women-led peace organization CODEPINK, which I cofounded with Jodie Evans after the 9/11 attacks, I have spent much of the last decade standing up against U.S. military intervention in the Middle East and supporting local democracy activists. I traveled many times to the region, listening to human rights advocates, marching with them in the streets, dodging tear gas and bullets, and getting beaten up and deported by government thugs.

I have seen, firsthand, the deadly effects of U.S. foreign policies. The 2003 U.S. invasion of Iraq destroyed the lives of millions, including many of my dear friends, and unleashed the sectarian hatred that later gave birth to the Islamic State. I recall a conversation with my Iraqi colleague Yanar Mohammad, daughter of a Shiite father and Sunni mother, and founder of the Organization of Women's Freedom in Iraq. When I asked her what was the most notable legacy of the U.S. invasion of her country, she gave the chilling response: "We, Sunnis and Shia, learned to hate each other."

In another part of the Middle East, U.S. military support for Israel has wreaked havoc on the lives of Palestinians and aroused the ire of people throughout the region. Continuous U.S. military interventions—from drone warfare in Yemen to overthrowing Muammar Gaddafi in Libya to funneling an endless stream of weapons into the region—have unleashed new levels of violence.

But the United States is not the only nation whose massive footprint has been trampling on the lives of people in the Middle East. The other nation is Saudi Arabia, an oppressive monarchy that denies human rights to its own people and exports extremism around the world. It also happens to be the closest U.S. ally in the Arab world.

During the 1980s and 1990s, I met intolerant and violent young men in Pakistan and Afghanistan who were trained to hate Westerners in Saudi schools. In 2001, I saw my own nation convulsed by an attack on September 11 that was perpetrated mostly by Saudis. It's not hard to connect the dots between the spread of the Saudi intolerant ideology of Wahhabism, the creation of Al Qaeda and the Islamic State, and the attacks in New York, Paris, Brussels, and San Bernadino.

You can also connect the dots between Saudi Arabia and the failure of some of the historic democratic uprisings associated with the Arab Spring, since the Saudi monarchy did not want calls for democracy to threaten its own grip on power. I was in Bahrain after Saudi tanks crushed the inspiring grassroots encampment in Pearl Square, where tens of thousands had gathered day after day to demand democracy. I will never forget the excitement of being in Tahrir Square during the Egyptian revolution, then watching, aghast, as a military coup backed by the Saudis put some forty thousand activists behind bars. In Yemen, the Saudis took a direct military role in that nation's internal conflict with a ruthless bombing campaign.

When I travel overseas, people often ask me why Saudi Arabia—a country that is so repressive internally and overseas—is such a close ally of the United States. Iranian friends want to know why the U.S. government is so outspoken about human rights violations in Iran but silent about worse abuses in the Saudi Kingdom. Yemenis ask why my government supplies weapons to the very nation— Saudi Arabia—that bombed their schools and hospitals. Saudi women ask why the United States, which professes great democratic values, props up a regime that treats women as second class citizens.

The easy answer is oil, weapons sales, and other business interests. Oil has formed the basis for Saudi–U.S. ties; the kingdom has become the largest purchaser of American weapons in the world, and hundreds of billions of Saudi petrodollars help shore up the U.S. economy. But there's another reason, perhaps more critical than any of the others: the American people have not demanded an end to this dysfunctional, toxic relationship. Why? In part, because they know so little about it.

Even Americans who consider themselves part of a peace movement know virtually nothing about the kingdom. The Saudi press is muzzled, foreign journalists are strictly monitored, and only tourists visiting for religious purposes are allowed in. Add to that a Saudi lobby that lines the pockets of U.S. think tanks such as the Middle East Institute, Ivy League universities such as Harvard and Yale, and influential institutions from the Clinton Foundation to the Carter Center. This checkbook diplomacy helps put a happy face on the abusive monarchy and silence its critics.

So we have a lot to uncover. This book is meant to be a primer, giving readers a basic understanding of how the kingdom holds on to power internally and how it tries to influence the outside world. It looks at the founding of the Saudi state; the treatment of dissidents, religious minorities, women, and migrant workers; the spread of Wahhabism; the kingdom's relationship with the West and its role in the region; and what the future might hold.

As we delve into the inner workings of this dystopian regime, don't mistake criticism of Saudi Arabia for Islamophobia. This book is not a critique of Islam but a critique of three intertwining factors that have shaped the Saudi nation: the extremist interpretation of Sunni Islam known as Wahhabism, the appropriation of the Saudi state by one family, and the Western support for this dynasty.

Criticizing Saudi Arabia should also not be equated with support for Saudi's nemesis: Iran. The Iranian government is guilty of some of the same abuses as the Saudis, such as restricting freedom of speech and assembly, imprisoning dissidents, and executing people for nonviolent offenses. But U.S. policy constantly rewards the Saudis while punishing Iran, even though the Iranian people have made significantly more progress than the Saudis in reforming their nation.

As outsiders, particularly those of us from North America and Europe, our responsibility is not to take sides in the Saudi/Iran split or Sunni/Shia sectarian divisions. Our responsibility is also not to change the Saudi regime; that is the job of the Saudi people. Many brave Saudis have been tweeting, blogging, marching, defying government restrictions, risking prison, and even sacrificing their lives to change their government. Our responsibility is to support these activists or, at the very least, to make sure our governments get out of their way as they attempt to transform their own nation.

CHAPTER 1: THE FOUNDING OF THE SAUDI STATE

Saudi Arabia gets its name from the Arabian Peninsula and from a single family: the Al Saud dynasty. It's the only country in the modern world to be named after a ruling family. This family, along with the dominance of an extremist religious sect and the discovery of oil, are key to understanding the kingdom today.

WHAT ARE THE ORIGINS OF SAUDI ARABIA?

Saudi Arabia traces its roots to a mid–eighteenth century alliance between a tribal leader and a conservative cleric.

The cleric was Sheikh Muhammed ibn Abd-al-Wahhab from the Najd province in central Arabia, where he studied Islamic law under the tutelage of his grandfather before going abroad to study in Medina, as well as in Iraq and Iran. He returned to Najd to preach a return to "pure," fundamentalist Islam that employed a literal interpretation of the Quran. Al-Wahhab believed in restoring the oneness of God and discarding the practices of praying to saints or venerating shrines, tombs, and other traditional sacred sites. He said people who participated in such misguided forms of worship were not only committing a sin, but were not real Muslims. His teachings have been characterized as puritanical, insisting that the original grandeur of Islam could be regained if the community would return to the original principles of the Prophet Muhammad, as al-Wahhab interpreted them.

The cleric found little support for his intolerant ideas until 1744, when he found a patron in tribal leader Muhammad Ibn Saud. Ibn Saud, head of the powerful Al Saud family in southern Najd, ruled a part of the Arabian Peninsula that had never fallen under control of the Ottoman Empire. He made a deal to endorse al-Wahhab's austere form of Islam and protect him from religious persecution; in exchange, the Al Saud family would get political legitimacy and regular income in the form of a tithe that al-Wahhab received from his followers. This union of political power and religious authority was also sealed by the marriage of Ibn Saud's son Abdulaziz to al-Wahhab's daughter.

The Al Saud family used the Wahhabi doctrine, now known as Wahhabism, to raid and rob neighboring villages under the guise of religious *jihad* (struggle). Ibn Saud and al-Wahhab also made use of the idea of martyrdom, insisting that those killed in battles to spread the faith were granted immediate entry into paradise. Conquered inhabitants were given the choice to convert or be killed.

Ibn Saud died in 1765, but his sons continued the conquest. By 1790, they controlled most of the Arabian Peninsula.

In 1801, they attacked the Shia holy city of Karbala, massacring thousands and destroying revered Shiite shrines. They also razed shrines in Mecca and Medina, erasing centuries of Islamic architecture because of the Wahhabist belief that these treasures represented idol worship. The sheer level of destruction provoked the wrath of the Sultan of the Ottoman Empire and in 1812, he dispatched the Egyptian Ottoman army to fight the Saudis. Outnumbered and under-equipped, the Saudis were defeated and forced into exile in Kuwait.

It was not until 1902 that the new Al Saud family leader, Abdulaziz Ibn Saud, returned from exile. Starting out with a small group of about sixty bedouin warriors called Ikhwan, he returned to conquer Riyadh (the nation's capital today). Drawing once again on the religious mission of Wahhabism, Abdulaziz recruited more warriors and took over province after province across the vast Arabian Peninsula. In 1924 he captured Mecca and a year later Medina, making him the ruler of the Two Holy Cities of Islam.

Abdulaziz declared himself king and in 1932, gave his family's name to the kingdom: Saudi Arabia.

The new nation was formed with a distinct division of power: the radical Wahhabi religious establishment would control the mosques, culture, and education, while the Al Saud family controlled key political functions, such as royal succession, foreign policies, and the armed forces.

Abdulaziz had a clever plan for keeping the new kingdom united: he married a daughter from every major tribe and influential religious family. Since the Quran says men can have only four wives, he married, then divorced, and then married again.

In total, he had more than twenty wives, about forty-five sons, and an unknown number of daughters.

With his copious flock of offspring, Abdulaziz slowly took power away from his brothers and cousins to elevate his own sons to positions of power. He then arranged for his sons to make similar kinds of marriages to powerful families. His family became known as the "royal family," and six of his sons—Kings Saud, Faisal, Khalid, Fahd, Abdullah, and Salman—have succeeded him as rulers of the Saudi Kingdom during the subsequent eight decades.

Abdulaziz died in 1953 and is officially recognized as the nation's founder. New kings are chosen from among his sons and their male descendants, normally by order of age. The king, in counsel with the royal inner circle, usually designates an heir apparent (the one immediately younger than him) who serves as crown prince; upon the king's death, the crown prince assumes the throne.

This transition of power does not always go smoothly. In 1964, when senior members of the royal family felt that King Saud was leading the country to the brink of economic collapse, they—together with the religious authorities—forced him into exile. Even worse, in 1975 King Faisal was assassinated by one of his nephews.

In 2015, King Salman ended the brother-to-brother succession by appointing his nephew, Mohammad bin Nayef, as crown prince and his young son, Mohammed bin Salman, as deputy crown prince. Crown Prince bin Nayef is the first grandson of Abdulaziz to be in line for the throne.

WHO HAS POWER IN THE KINGDOM?

There are over ten thousand Saudi princes, but the majority of the power and wealth is in the hands of about two hundred male descendants of King Abdulaziz. The royal family is often divided by factions based on clan loyalties, personal ambitions, and ideological differences about the speed of reform and the role of the religious leaders.

As one of world's last absolute monarchs, the Saudi king has ultimate authority in virtually every key aspect of government. The king is the prime minister and commander-in-chief. He appoints senior government officials, the provincial governors, ambassadors, and other foreign envoys. Legislation is enacted either by royal decree or by ministerial decree, which has to be approved by the king. The king even acts as the final court of appeal and has the power of pardon.

There is no constitution. The law of the land is *Sharia* (Islamic law). The Quran and the *Sunnah* (the traditions and practices of the Prophet Muhammad) are considered the country's constitution and are subject to interpretation by the *ulema,* the religious leaders. The ulema has a direct role in government, from approving the appointment of the king and royal decrees to enforcing the nation's moral and social rules. Other powerful players in Saudi society are tribal leaders and wealthy business families.

No political parties are permitted, and there are no national elections. In 1953, King Saud established the Council of Ministers with twenty-two ministries—all appointed by the king. Key ministries like Defense, Interior, and Foreign Affairs are usually held by members of the royal family, as are most of the thirteen governorships.

In 1992, King Fahd created a new political body, the *Majiis Al-Shura*, or Shura Council, which is a consultative body of 150 members appointed by the king for four-year terms that can be renewed. The Shura Council can propose legislation but has no legislative powers.

The nation's only elected bodies (really, semi-elected) are the municipal councils. The first municipal council elections were held in 2005, and half the council seats were appointed, half elected (but only by men). The second election was held in 2011. In the third election in 2015, two-thirds of the seats were opened up for elections and for the first time, women were allowed to vote and run for office. These municipal councils, while hailed by Saudi's Western allies as a great democratic leap forward, have no legislative power and focus only on local issues, such as maintenance of infrastructure and trash collection.

WHAT IS THE ROLE OF OIL?

Saudi Arabia is a nation built by oil. Oil has not only determined domestic development, but also endowed the conservative dynasty with an oversized global influence. As Toby Craig Jones noted in *Desert Kingdom*: "Oil turned out to be not just a prized natural resource that generated great wealth; it also generated a set of relations among politics, big business, global capital, labor, and scientific expertise, all of which interacted to form the modern state of Saudi Arabia."[1]

Saudi Arabia has about 16 percent of the world's proven oil reserves (second only to Venezuela), ranks as the world's largest oil exporter, and plays a leading role in OPEC (the Organization of Petroleum Exporting Countries). The petroleum sector accounts for over 80 percent of export earnings.[2]

Saudi's oil story dates back to 1933, when Standard Oil of California (now Chevron) won a concession to explore for oil in eastern Saudi Arabia. After several years of failed efforts, in 1938 the drillers were successful beyond their wildest dreams, discovering the largest source of crude oil the world had seen. Standard Oil, along with three partners that would later become Texaco, Exxon, and Mobil, established the Arabian American Oil Company, or Aramco. The Saudi government was a partner in the company, and over the years purchased more and more shares. In 1980 it purchased 100 percent of the company and changed its name to Saudi Aramco.

Saudi Aramco produces about ten million barrels of oil a day, which is more than the domestic output of all U.S. oil companies combined. It also owns a global chain of refineries and petro-chemical facilities, as well as the world's fourth largest natural gas reserves. To manage this vast empire, it employs about fifty-five thousand people, including thousands of Americans who work in the kingdom and live in special compounds for foreigners.

While Aramco's total value is treated like a state secret, it is considered the richest company in the world. "By any measure,

Saudi Arabian Oil Co. is in a league of its own," said Bloomberg News.[3] According to *Forbes*, Aramco generates more than $1 billion a day in revenue. That's right—$1 billion a day! Its total value is many times the largest private oil company, Exxon, which had a market value of $344 billion on April 1, 2016. Aramco's value has been estimated at anywhere between $1.25 trillion and $10 trillion. By comparison, on April 1, 2016, two of the world's wealthiest companies, Apple and Google, were worth $610 billion and $516 billion, respectively.

Of course, Aramco's revenue, like those of all oil companies, depends on the price of oil, a factor that can fluctuate wildly depending on supply, demand, and world events. Prices spiked during the 1990 Gulf War as buyers worried about supply. They dove from $143 a barrel to just $30 during the 2008 U.S. financial crisis. After rising again to $112 in 2014, two years later a global drop in consumption and a glut of oil on the market sent prices tumbling back down to $30 again.

Low oil prices are a boon to consumers but are disastrous for oil-producing countries. Saudi Oil Minister Ali al-Naimi said in 2015 that the government did not expect oil prices to rebound in the near future but that Saudi Arabia, due to its low production costs and its hefty financial reserves, was positioned to weather the low prices better than other producers.

The Saudi strategy to beat the competition was to keep pumping cheap oil, forcing out high-cost producers like U.S. and Canadian companies that were exploiting shale, oil sands, and deep-sea resources. Flooding the market was also a way to hurt other oil-producing countries, such as Iran and Russia—countries that were not only Saudi competitors but political adversaries.

While the Saudis were indeed better positioned than most oil producers to ride out the pricing storms, they, too, have been pummeled by low prices and will run up budget deficits for the foreseeable future.

The volatility of the market, the inevitability of dwindling oil reserves, the threat of catastrophic climate change, and the increased global awareness about the need to cut carbon emissions—all these factors put into question the viability of an economic model based almost entirely on fossil fuels.

Recognizing this looming crisis, in May 2016 Deputy Crown Prince Mohammed bin Salman announced an ambitious agenda, called Vision 2030, aimed at overhauling the structure of the economy to dramatically increase non-oil revenue, reduce spending by lowering subsidies, and encourage more foreign investment. The plan would raise funds by selling off part of the oil giant Aramco and investing the proceeds in a broad range of assets around the world. It remains to be seen how much of this plan will actually be implemented.

HOW IS THE OIL MONEY DISTRIBUTED?

Before oil was discovered in Saudi Arabia in 1938, most Saudis lived a humble, austere life in the desert. They made their living as nomadic herdsmen, traders, farmers, and, along the coasts, as fishermen and pearl divers. Others provided services to pilgrims traveling to the holy cities of Mecca and Medina.

Thanks to oil, Saudi Arabia was transformed into one of the richest countries in the world. In 2014, it was ranked the world's nineteenth largest economy, with the eighth highest per capita GDP.

In the 1960s and early 1970s, with billions in oil revenue pouring in and a tiny population of about four million, the government began investing in education and providing a generous package of welfare benefits to its citizens. It also began a frenzy of hiring foreign contractors to build everything from communications systems, transportation infrastructure, and refineries to hospitals, universities, and housing projects.

With its massive oil wealth, Saudi Arabia created a large middle class that lived off the benefits of the welfare state and paid no personal taxes. But the royals have always seen the nation's oil as their personal treasure rather than the patrimony of all Saudis. While they have distributed some of profits, they've kept enormous amounts for themselves, producing one of the highest concentrations of super rich in the world.

The royals line their pockets through a web of nepotism, corruption, bloated commissions, and no-bid government contracts they award to themselves. The lines between personal wealth and state assets are blurred. King Abdullah's personal fortune was estimated at $18 billion in 2012 and King Salman's worth in 2016 was estimated at $17 billion.

Senior princes often commingle their assets with their government portfolios, and then appoint their sons to senior positions so the wealth and power stay in the family. Other get-rich schemes include confiscating private land or claiming land that no one owns, then selling it to the government at exorbitant prices.

The biggest royal corruption scandal was the $2 billion in kickbacks—yes, that's billion, not million—paid by the UK military company BAE Systems to former Saudi ambassador to the United States Prince Bandar bin Sultan. Since some of the funds had been funneled through a U.S. bank, the U.S. Department of Justice launched an investigation that forced BAE to pay nearly $450 million in penalties, one of the largest fines in the history of the Department of Justice. However, Prince Bandar, known as Bush Bandar for his close relationship with George Bush, faced no charges in the United States even though he is the one who received this monumental bribe. He also faced no charges in the UK. Prime Minister Tony Blair halted the investigations into the corruption scandal after the Saudis threatened "repercussions," including withholding intelligence information. [4]

To the disgust of the nation's religious leaders, Saudi princes became notorious big spenders in Europe's casinos. King Fahd, before he was king, was photographed in a Monte Carlo casino on an evening when he gambled away $6 million. The princes also became notorious for their lavish lifestyles at home. Alcohol is banned inside the kingdom, but parties by Saudi princes are infamous for their liquor, cocaine, and prostitutes. Many royal residences have basement bars, discos, and clubs catering to a growing demand among the young Saudi elite for Western-style entertainment inside the kingdom.

Cables leaked by WikiLeaks in 2010, written by the U.S. Consul General in Jeddah, revealed the gaping double standards. "Behind the façade of Wahhabi conservatism in the streets, the underground nightlife for Jeddah's elite youth is thriving and throbbing.... The full range of worldly temptations and vices are available—alcohol, drugs, sex—but strictly behind closed doors. The religious police keep their distance from parties hosted by the royals." Another cable noted: "Saudi youth get to enjoy relative social freedom and indulge fleshy pursuits, but only behind closed doors—and only the rich."[5]

The richest man in Saudi Arabia is Prince Al-Waleed bin Talal, a grandson of the nation's founder and nephew of King Abdullah. He became a billionaire through investments, many of them in American companies from Citigroup and Disney to eBay and Apple. His main palace in Riyadh has 420 rooms adorned with 1,500 tons of Italian marble, 250 TVs, gold-plated faucets, several swimming pools—and portraits of himself. He has his own Boeing 747 and Airbus 321, a 280-foot yacht (once owned by Donald Trump), and a 120-acre farm outside Riyadh with 5 artificial lakes and a zoo.

In 2013, *Forbes* magazine estimated his fortune at $20 billion. But the prince was not happy with *Forbes*; in fact, he sued them. Why? They said he was worth a mere $20 billion instead of $30 billion, denying him a place among the world's top ten richest people. In 2015, *Forbes* did list him as being worth close to $30 billion, but by then others had surpassed him, making the poor prince only the thirty-fourth richest man in the world.

IS THERE POVERTY IN THE KINGDOM?

Aside from the super-rich, there is a significant middle class, many of whom work in the government's huge bureaucracy and receive good salaries. The government employs three million people, with an average salary in 2015 of $2,400 a month, or $28,800 annually.[6]

But there are also millions of poor Saudis and migrant workers who struggle on the fringes of one of the world's most powerful economies. Jobs and welfare programs have failed to keep pace with a population that has soared from six million in 1970 to twenty-eight million by 2012 to thirty-one million in 2016.

Unemployment is higher than one might suspect in the oil-rich nation, particularly among the youth. Two-thirds of the population are under thirty, and the youth unemployment rate is roughly 30 percent.[7] Some 1.8 million Saudis are enrolled with *Hafiz*, the country's unemployment benefits program.

The government discloses little official data about its poorest citizens. For many years, officials actually denied the existence of poverty. That changed in 2002, when Crown Prince Abdullah visited a slum with the Minister of Social Affairs and a film crew. When the story was aired on state television, it was the first time many well-off Saudis became aware of poverty in their country.

Time magazine photographer Lynsey Addario is one of the few Western reporters allowed to photograph the seamy side of the nation's capital. In her 2013 article "Rich Nation, Poor People," she wrote: "What you see on the surface are the shiny buildings and the shopping malls and the new universities being built—the wealthy side. I was actually quite shocked when we went to the slums." She met families living in overcrowded, cockroach-infested houses in the heart of Riyadh, struggling to pay their bills. She reported that an estimated 20 percent of the population, if not more, lives in crippling poverty.[8]

Open discussion of poverty is still taboo. In 2011, two Saudi video bloggers made a ten-minute documentary on poverty in the capital, including interviews with beggars, barefoot children, and a man who supported twenty relatives on a salary of $666 a month. The video was viewed online by over a million people. Six days after it was posted, the government arrested the young filmmakers, held them for two weeks, and censored the video.

The poorest families are often headed by women who are widowed, divorced, or have disabled husbands. Some women in polygamous marriages find themselves descending into poverty because their husbands can't afford the financial burden of maintaining more than one household. Women trying to live without a man's income are handicapped by the strict religious and cultural obstacles placed on women working outside the home.

Many migrant workers live in poverty, as do the approximately seventy thousand descendants of nomadic tribes who live like stateless people. Their uncertain legal status makes it difficult for them to receive government benefits.

Poverty is also widespread in the oil-rich Eastern Province, where the Shia minority live. For decades people in that region have protested, at great risk to their lives, the skewed distribution of oil resources. One underground activist said in the documentary *Saudi's Secret Uprising*, "The biggest oil field in the world is in our home, Qatif, but what do we find here? Dilapidated houses, poverty, hunger, and marginalization."[9]

HOW HAS THE GOVERNMENT ADDRESSED POVERTY?

The government spends billions of dollars each year on pensions and benefits for the elderly and disabled, and subsidies for the poor. Funds to help the poor also come from the Islamic system of *zakat*, a religious obligation in which individuals and companies donate 2.5 percent of their income to charity. There is also a tradition where royal family members periodically hold court to meet people seeking help. The process, however, is not open to all citizens and the meetings are irregular. While they afford some Saudis a rare opportunity to get assistance from the powerful, they also reinforce the arbitrary and personalized nature of wealth and power.

In 2012, responding to the fear of an Arab Spring uprising in Saudi Arabia, King Abdullah announced plans to spend an additional $37 billion on housing, wage increases, unemployment benefits, and other social programs. When King Salman became the new monarch in 2015, he bought the goodwill of much of the population by announcing bonuses worth two months of salary for all government workers, pensioners, soldiers, and students on government stipends. State-run media showed grateful Saudis jumping for joy and praising the king. "Saudis are spending," announced the *New York Times*. "Some have treated themselves to new cellphones, handbags, and trips abroad. They have paid off debts, given to charity and bought gold necklaces for their mothers. Some men have set aside money to marry a first, second or third wife." The author added, "So, for the moment, there is little talk about human rights abuses or political reform."[10]

Despite government attempts to buy the allegiance of its citizens, people remain angry over the skewed distribution of the nation's resources and the rising cost of living. In September 2013, a discussion using an Arabic hashtag that loosely translates as "the salary does not meet my needs" exploded on Twitter. It reached seventeen million tweets in the first two weeks and became the most popular hashtag in Arabic.

The anger expressed on Twitter was fueled by growing unemployment and frustration at government spending overseas, including the announcement that the government would give billions of dollars in financial aid to the Egyptian regime of Abdul Fattah al-Sisi that came to power in a 2013 military coup.

"The government is giving handouts to Egypt, Jordan, and Tunisia. Meanwhile, Saudis are paying most of their salaries on rent, private schools, private hospitals—because public ones aren't good. Meanwhile, salaries have practically stayed the same," said Saudi activist Manal al-Sharif.[11] This anger can be expected to grow since, in 2016, with falling oil prices and rising deficits, the government cut benefits and raised the price of everything from fuel to electricity to water.

Of course, if the Saudi government didn't spend such a huge amount of money on its military, it would have a lot more money to invest in its own people. In 2015, the military ate up 25 percent of the total budget, double what was spent on health and social development.[12]

WHAT IS THE ROLE OF RELIGION IN DAILY LIFE?

The clerics have a much greater role in Saudi society than in other Islamic countries. They control the mosques, education ministry, justice ministry, Islamic affairs ministry, and religious police force.

Many aspects of daily life are defined by religion. Much of the education in the schools and the broadcasts on state television are devoted to religious issues. Five times a day, Saudis are called to prayer from the minarets of thousands of mosques scattered throughout the country.

Restrictions on dress and social behavior are strictly enforced. Saudi Arabia is one of the few countries that have "religious police," officially known as the Commission for the Propagation of Virtue and the Elimination of Vice, but also referred to as *Mutaween* (the pious) or *hay'a* (the committee). There are about four thousand religious police. They patrol the streets enforcing the Saudi interpretation of Sharia, such as dress codes, the strict separation of unrelated men and women, the ban on alcohol, and the observance of prayer. They detain and berate offenders, and make sure that businesses are shut down during prayer time.

The religious police have been infamous over the years for committing terrible abuses. They once beat a man to death for having alcohol in his home; they kept a woman in solitary confinement for sitting alone in the back of a taxi; they raided a private home to arrest a priest for celebrating mass. One of the worst tragedies was in 2002, when an accidental fire broke out in a girls' school. The religious police stopped the girls from leaving the burning building because they were not wearing their *abayas* (black outer garments). When the girls ran back inside the building to get their garments, many suffocated and fifteen of them died.[13]

Throughout the years, the power of the religious police has risen and fallen, depending on political circumstances and the king in power. When more liberal kings have been in power, they have tried to curb the authority of the religious police. In a 2013 reform under King Abdullah, the religious police were no longer supposed to detain people, make arrests, conduct interrogations, carry out warrantless searches, guard the entrances to shopping malls to enforce "proper dress code," or bar women from malls if they were not accompanied by a male guardian. Arrests were only supposed to be made in the presence of the regular police.

But the new rules were constantly broken. In February 2016, a video captured an incident in which the religious police stopped two young women on a street in Riyadh and ordered them to cover their faces and get into their car, but they refused. While one of the women escaped, they chased the other woman, then shoved and dragged her on the ground. In 2015, the religious police raided Riyadh's Marina Mall, tearing down from the displays any abayas that weren't black. In another incident, they took the ridiculous measure of arresting a life-sized female doll being used as a mascot by a candy store. Why? There was a man inside the doll, and the religious police insisted that Sharia law prohibits a man from pretending to be a woman.

King Abdullah's successor, King Salman, issued new rules in 2016 to curb the religious police, denying them the authority to arrest, pursue, or request ID cards from suspects. The new regulations also require the religious police to clearly display official ID cards containing their name, position, branch, and official work hours. They still have the authority, however, to enforce sex segregation rules in public spaces.

Curiously, while Saudi religious authorities are obsessed with modesty, this doesn't translate into calls for simple lifestyles. Massive shopping malls full of brand-name stores are a Saudi staple. "Oddly enough, Wahhabism has no problem with rampant consumerism and capitalism, or American fast-food restaurants, commercial malls, or luxury hotels. The Wahhabi Muslim is pushed to buy electronics, invest in the stock market, consume American fast food, but not to think," said *Islamic Utopia* author Andrew Hammond.[14]

MEDEA BENJAMIN

WHAT IS THE SIGNIFICANCE OF SAUDI ARABIA'S ROLE AS THE HOST OF MECCA, MEDINA, AND THE HAJJ PILGRIMAGE?

Saudi Arabia's power in the world is from not just its oil wealth. It also comes from the fact that it is home to the holy shrines of Mecca and Medina. Many Muslims around the world resent that a nation dominated by the Wahhabi version of Islam is now the guardian of Islam's holiest sites.

For a thousand years, the city of Mecca was the center of Sufism, the most spiritual and mystic form of Islam. Music, dance, ecstatic prayer, and celebration marked the gatherings of the divine and the faithful at the shrines of saints. When the Wahhabi backed House of Saud took control of Mecca in 1924, in less than a hundred years they erased that rich, mystic past.

The Saudis regard reverence for religious or historic sites as a form of idolatry, so they unceremoniously bulldozed these ancient treasures, including five of the original seven mosques built in Mecca soon after the Prophet Muhammad's death. The home of the Prophet's first wife, Khadijah, is today the site of public toilets. The house of the first caliph, Abu Bakr, is a Hilton Hotel. The Grand Mosque in Mecca is now overshadowed by the massive, postmodern Clock Royal Tower, the third tallest building in the world, built by the Bin Laden Group at a cost of $15 billion.[15]

According to the UK-based Islamic Heritage Research Foundation, over 98 percent of the kingdom's historical and religious sites have been demolished.[16] The destruction reflects not only the Wahhabi doctrine, but also the need to accommodate massive numbers of religious visitors. As the population of many Muslim countries has grown tenfold in the past century, the number of pilgrims flocking to Mecca every year has risen to about four million.

Most of these visitors arrive during the annual pilgrimage called the *Hajj*, which is the largest gathering of humanity anywhere in the world. All devout Muslims—as long as they are in good health, can afford to make the trip, and support their families while they are away—are supposed to perform this religious duty at least once in their lives to demonstrate their solidarity with the Muslim people and their submission to God.

About 45 percent of all pilgrims are Saudis; the rest come from other countries. A 2012 Pew Research Center survey found that 9 percent of Muslims worldwide had performed the Hajj, but this varied greatly from country to country based on proximity to Mecca, wealth, degree of religiosity, and access to visas.[17]

The pilgrimages are big business for the kingdom, bringing in about $8.5 billion every year. To accommodate all these visitors and the growth of Mecca and Medina, the Saudis have spent about $100 billion on airport, hotel, and road infrastructure.

Despite their huge investment, there have been scores of deadly incidents during the Hajj, including stampedes, collapsing cranes (118 people were killed in 2015), tent fires, and crumbling hotels. In 1987, a tragedy with international repercussions occurred. In the 1980s, Iranian pilgrims had established a

MEDEA BENJAMIN

tradition of holding demonstrations against the United States and Israel during the Hajj. In the 1987 protest, the marchers were confronted by Saudi riot police and National Guardsmen. When the demonstrators tried to push through police lines, the Saudi forces opened fire, causing a stampede among demonstrators and other pilgrims. The death toll was 402 people: 275 Iranians, 85 Saudis, and 42 other pilgrims.

The Saudi government denied that its forces had opened fire on the pilgrims, a serious violation of the sanctity of the holy city, but the Iranian government showed foreign journalists the corpses of many Iranians killed by gunfire.

Even worse in terms of numbers killed was the catastrophic stampede in 2015, when at least 2,200 people died. The Saudi Interior Ministry stated that the stampede was triggered when two large groups of pilgrims intersected from different directions onto the same street. Adding to the crisis of intense overcrowding was the extreme heat of about 110 degrees, which was the hottest temperature in Mecca in twenty years. Mismanagement by the Saudi authorities and a poor rescue response complicated the situation.

There were unconfirmed reports that a convoy of 200 soldiers and 150 police officers escorting Deputy Crown Prince Mohammad bin Salman triggered the disaster by blocking a street, forcing pilgrims to turn around against the flow of traffic.

The incident caused an international scandal because of all the foreigners who lost their lives. Over four hundred of the dead were from Iran, which led the Iranian government to announce that in 2016 its citizens would not participate in the Hajj.

To deal with the overwhelming crowds, the Saudi government has introduced a new visa system that prioritizes first-time pilgrims to Mecca over repeat visitors. But the recurrence of such deadly incidents has tarnished the Saudis' image as guardians of the holy sites and has drawn widespread criticism from around the Muslim world.

Safety concerns aside, there is a more basic dilemma facing the Muslim world. Should a kingdom founded on such a narrow interpretation of Islam have a stranglehold over access to the holiest sites of a religion that has thrived on traditions of diversity and tolerance for over a thousand years?

CHAPTER 2: A RELIGIOUS STATE WITHOUT FREEDOM OF RELIGION

The Kingdom of Saudi Arabia is a theocratic monarchy in which Sunni Islam is the official—and only—state religion. Specifically, it is the Sunni branch of Islam as interpreted by the eighteenth-century religious scholar Muhammad ibn Abd al-Wahhab. Outside Saudi Arabia, this branch of Islam is often referred to as "Wahhabism." Some Saudis claim that the term is derogatory and prefer the term "Salafism" instead.

One might assume that a religious state would guarantee religious freedom to its citizens, but the reality in this theocracy is quite the opposite.

Year after year, the U.S. government's Commission on International Religious Freedom gives Saudi Arabia its worst ranking: Tier 1 Country of Particular Concern. This is reserved for countries that commit "systematic, ongoing and egregious violations of religious freedom," including Sudan, North Korea, and Burma.[1]

WHAT RIGHT TO WORSHIP DO NON-MUSLIMS HAVE?

There is no religious freedom for non-Muslims. There are eight to ten million foreigners working in Saudi Arabia. They represent a variety of religions, such as Christianity, Hinduism, Buddhism, and Sikhism, but the public practice of any religion other than Islam is banned.

Saudi Arabia is the only state in the world to ban all churches and any other non-Muslim houses of worship. In 2005 King Abdullah said that allowing non-Muslim places of worship in Saudi Arabia would be like "asking the Vatican to build a mosque inside of it."[2] The comparison is ludicrous since the Vatican is a tiny city-state of 450 Catholics tucked inside Rome, whereas Saudi Arabia is a nation of thirty million inhabited by millions of non-Muslims, including over two million Christian foreign workers.

Non-Muslims are not allowed to worship in public places, but the Saudi government is supposed to protect their right to private worship, including gathering in homes for religious practice. This right is not always respected and is not codified in law, leaving worshippers at risk of abuse by the religious police. Indeed, non-Muslim worshippers have been arrested, imprisoned, and flogged for engaging in overt religious activity. Foreign residents arrested for such "crimes" are usually deported, sometimes after enduring lengthy periods of detention.[3]

In 2014, Saudi authorities stormed the house where a group was worshipping, after neighbors reported that the house had been converted into a church. Twenty-seven people were arrested, and numerous Bibles and musical instruments were reportedly confiscated.

Until March 2004, the official government website stated that Jews were forbidden from entering the country. As of December 2014, the Saudi Labor Ministry website says that foreign workers of various faiths, including Judaism, are allowed to live and work in Saudi Arabia, unless they are Israeli or affiliated with Israel. They are still not allowed to publicly practice their religion, and no one with an Israeli government stamp on his or her passport is allowed into the kingdom.

Non-Muslim clergy are not allowed to visit the country for the purpose of conducting religious services, although some enter the country under other auspices and perform religious functions in secret. Proselytizing by non-Muslims, including the distribution of religious materials such as Bibles, is illegal. Customs officials are known to open packages and cargo to search for Bibles and non-Muslim religious videotapes, and these materials are subject to confiscation.

Saudi law prohibits alcoholic beverages and pork products in the country, as they are considered counter to Islam. Those caught with these products (with the exception of diplomats) may receive harsh punishments.

Non-Muslims are not allowed to hold Saudi citizenship, while children born to Muslim fathers are automatically considered

Muslim, regardless of the religious tradition in which they were raised.

Insulting or showing contempt for Sunni Islam is punishable by death, although the more common penalty is a long prison sentence. Conversion from Islam to another religion is considered apostasy, which is also punishable by death. In February 2015, the Saudi courts sentenced a man to death for apostasy after he filmed himself tearing up a copy of the Quran. This case was particularly embarrassing since when the sentence was handed down, Deputy Crown Prince Mohammed bin Nayef was on an official visit to England trying to whitewash his nation's image.[4]

The 2014 terrorism law made religious dissent even more dangerous. It classifies blasphemy, advocating atheism, and questioning the fundamentals of the Islamic religion as terrorist acts that could result in a prison term of up to twenty years.

Sharia law applies to all people inside Saudi Arabia, regardless of their beliefs. Judges may ignore or discount the testimony of people who are not practicing Muslims or Muslims who do not adhere to the official Sunni interpretation of Islam. While the law states that all defendants should be treated equally, crimes against Muslims may result in harsher penalties than crimes against non-Muslims.

All public school students at all levels must study Islamic religious education that conforms to the official version of Islam. If students don't want to study Islam, they must go to private schools.

Non-Muslims are strictly banned from the holy city of Mecca. There are checkpoints along the highways to Mecca. If the guards at a checkpoint suspect you might not be Muslim, they ask to see proof. The national IDs for Saudis and the visas issued to foreigners all indicate whether the bearer is Muslim. If non-Muslims somehow make it through to Mecca and are discovered, they can be jailed or deported.

WHAT ABOUT SUFI MUSLIMS?

Sufism is not a branch of Islam, but a practice; Sufis can be Shia or Sunni. In Saudi Arabia, Sufism, with its use of music, dance, meditation, and the teachings of Sufi masters, was denounced as heretical and banned since the time the kingdom was founded.

The 9/11 attacks, however, increased international scrutiny on the repressive nature of Wahhabism and led to more religious freedom for the Sufis. *Mawlids*, the Sufi celebrations of the birth and life of Muhammad, became permitted; Sufi books, cassettes, and DVDs became available for purchase, and traditional Sufi dress was reintroduced.

While there has been some progress, Sufis are still far from enjoying religious freedom and acceptance in the Wahhabi state. As Wasif Kabli, a fifty-nine-year-old Sufi businessman, said, "We were upgraded from infidels to people who are ignorant and practicing their religion wrong."[5]

WHAT'S THE DIFFERENCE BETWEEN SHIA AND SUNNI MUSLIMS, AND HOW ARE THE SHIA TREATED?

The split between Sunni and Shia first emerged after the death of the Prophet Muhammad in 632 A.D. The majority believed the new leader should be Abu Bakr, a friend of the Prophet and father of his wife Aisha. This group become known as the Sunnis and today make up about 80 percent of Muslims worldwide. The minority claimed the Prophet had anointed his cousin and son-in-law Ali to be his successor. They became known as Shia, a contraction of "*shiaat Ali*," or the partisans of Ali. The split deepened when Ali's son Imam Husayn was beheaded in 680 A.D. by Sunni troops. As time went on, the religious beliefs of the two groups became more and more divergent.

Between 10 and 15 percent of the Saudi population is Shia. Most live in the oil-rich Eastern Province. A very small group of Shia, about one hundred thousand, are called Ismailis and live in the southern region near Yemen. An even smaller group, about thirty-two thousand, are called Nakhawila and live in and around the city of Medina.

Ever since the Wahhabi expansion in the Arabian Peninsula in the mid-eighteenth century, the Shia in Saudi Arabia have endured state-sponsored discrimination, social marginalization, and campaigns of violence waged by anti-Shiite hardliners. According to Sarah Leah Whitson, Middle East and North Africa director at Human Rights Watch, "All the Saudi Shia want is for

MEDEA BENJAMIN

their government to respect their identity and treat them equally. Yet Saudi authorities routinely treat these people with scorn and suspicion."[6]

Many Saudis have been indoctrinated with a deep hate for Shiism. Wahhabis have been particularly hostile toward the Shiites. During the early nineteenth century, Wahhabis destroyed Shiite shrines at Mecca, Medina, and Karbala, accusing the Shiites of worshipping idols. Government-affiliated religious authorities regularly disparage Shia citizens, calling them unbelievers and puppets of Iran. The Saudi rulers benefit from this divide, as it keeps the two groups from uniting to demand reform. "What the regime fears most is any attempt to bridge the sectarian divide and unite Sunni and Shia activists around the issue of denied basic common rights," said Saudi scholar Madawi al-Rasheed.[7]

Shia are allowed to have their own mosques in Shia areas, but unlike Sunni mosques, the government does not pay for them. Shia are not allowed to build *hussainiyya*, prayer halls to commemorate the martyrdom of Imam Husayn. In Shia areas around the world, these houses are like community centers, used for religious rituals, prayers, social gatherings, and weddings. "We can't get an official permit to build a hussainiyya, so people usually start building it as if it were a house and then take down the interior walls," said an anonymous Shia source. "While the government builds huge Sunni mosques and centers all over the country and around the world, we have to hide what we are doing and scrape together private donations. It's not right."[8]

U.S. diplomatic cables in 2008 reported a campaign to close Shia mosques and prevent Shia celebrations, as well as ongoing arrests of people trying to take part in these celebrations. Mosques were closed on the pretext of permit violations and zoning issues; electricity was cut off and owners of the buildings were threatened with arrest.

Shia are also restricted in their ability to publicly display their faith. After much pressure, the authorities finally allowed the Shia in the Eastern Province to celebrate their major festival, Ashura, as long as the celebrants did not engage in large, public marches or the practice of self-flagellation. Their celebrations are monitored by the police.

There is also discrimination in the education system. Shia cannot teach religion in public schools and Shia pupils are told by Sunni teachers that they are infidels. According to scholar Vali Nasr, Saudi textbooks traditionally "characterize Shiism as a form of heresy . . . worse than Christianity and Judaism."[9] There are unofficial restrictions on the number of Shia admitted to universities, and Shia students generally cannot gain admission to military academies.

With the discovery of oil in the Eastern Province, the Shia got jobs as skilled and semiskilled workers, but they receive very little of the contracting and subcontracting wealth the industry generates. Shia are also discriminated against in government employment, especially in positions that relate to national security, such as the military, police, or the security services. There has been only one Shia minister (in 2014, King Abdullah appointed a Shia as Minister of State) and only a handful of Shia members have been appointed to the 150-seat Shura Council.

Shia face bias in the judiciary as well, where Sunni judges sometimes disqualify Shia witnesses on the basis of their religion and exclusively follow the tenets of Sunni religious law. In some courts, Shia are not allowed to be judges.

HOW HAS THE VIOLENCE THAT HAS WRACKED THE MIDDLE EAST AFFECTED SUNNI–SHIA RELATIONS INSIDE THE KINGDOM?

Sunni superiority and sectarian hatred not only are deeply held beliefs among Saudi rulers, but also are part of a strategy to maintain political and economic control. The result is a pernicious, everyday sectarianism that becomes more open and dangerous in times of regional upheaval and heightened tensions with Iran.

The 2003 U.S. invasion of Iraq and the subsequent rise of Iranian influence in the region inflamed Sunni–Shia tensions. The Saudi government sees any kind of dissent among the Shia as part of an Iranian conspiracy; the Shia are accused of being traitors who are loyal to Iran and trying to destabilize the kingdom. At the same time, Shia have been upset over the Saudi military interventions in Bahrain and Yemen that have killed so many of their fellow Shia.

The appearance of the Islamic State inside Saudi Arabia starting in 2015 has terrorized the Shia and further aggravated

Sunni–Shia relations. Islamic State supporters, who are Sunni, have attacked Shia mosques, mostly during Friday noon or midday prayers. Many Shiites fault Saudi officials for not protecting them. They also say that the kingdom's religious establishment has been sowing sectarian hatred for decades and is therefore also responsible for the attacks.

HAVE THE SHIA RISEN UP TO DEMAND THEIR RIGHTS?

There have been labor protests for decades in the Eastern Province, where, in the early days of Aramco, Shia oil workers were paid less than Sunnis. The government has a history of detaining and imprisoning Shia Muslims not only for participating in demonstrations and calling for reform, but also for holding religious gatherings in prayer halls, organizing religious events, and celebrating religious holidays.

In 1979, inspired by the Iranian revolution when the pro-Western Shah was replaced by a Shia government, Saudi Shia rose up, calling for more rights. When they performed their traditional Ashura processions in public, the government sent in twenty thousand soldiers to stop them. Three days of riots ensued, with cars burned, banks attacked, and shops looted. At least twenty-seven Shia were killed. The three-day riots turned into four months of intermittent demonstrations that eventually died out when the leaders were killed, detained, or went into hiding.[10]

Even then, Shia continued to press for their rights, and to be repressed. In 1990, Amnesty International published a report saying that from 1983 to 1990, over seven hundred political prisoners had been detained without charge or trial, most of them Shia.[11]

Another round of protests took place in February 2009, in what became known as the Al-Baqi' incident. Shia pilgrims going to Mecca for the anniversary of the Prophet Muhammad's death were attacked by Sunni religious police at the Al-Baqi' cemetery in Medina. A fifteen-year-old Shia pilgrim was shot in the chest, and a Shia sheikh was stabbed in the back. Shia in the Eastern Province demonstrated in solidarity. Security forces reacted by arresting scores of demonstrators, including children, and temporarily shutting down Shia places of worship.

During this time of heightened tensions, Saudi rulers and Shia leaders came together in an effort to improve relations. In 1993, a pact was signed with King Fahd and the government sent a massive assistance package to the Shia region, including large projects to upgrade the infrastructure and provide employment. In 2003, then–crown prince Abdullah started the National Dialogues initiative, which brought senior Sunni and Shia clerics together. When Abdullah became king in 2005, he advocated for tolerance between religions.

But discrimination by state institutions continued, and in 2011, inspired by the Arab Spring uprisings in Tunisia and Egypt, Shia took to the streets once again. During the protests, at least sixteen people died at the hands of government forces, sometimes during peaceful demonstrations and occasionally in violent exchanges with police. The protests initially began with demands for Shia rights and the release of political prisoners, but in the summer of 2012, as more lives were lost and their voices ignored, the demands turned into far-reaching calls for a constitution, popular participation in decision-making, and, in some instances, the overthrow of the regime.

The government stopped the media from reporting on the protests, even withdrawing the credentials from foreign journalists who covered them. It launched an extensive campaign to discredit the protesters via multiple media outlets. But videos and photos leaked out on the internet, showing that despite the ban on all demonstrations, hundreds of Shia were out on the streets—day after day—calling for the downfall of the Saudi ruling family.

Activists and leaders in the community were beaten and arrested; some were later executed. When Sheikh Nimr al-Nimr was executed in January 2016, the U.S. Commission on International Religious Freedom (USCIRF) said: "Sheikh al-Nimr's execution blatantly disregards the right to dissent and the right to religious freedom of Shia Muslims in the country and contributes to sectarian discord both within Saudi Arabia and in the region. It is long past due for the government of Saudi Arabia to honor international standards of justice and ensure the religious freedom and equal protection rights of everyone in the Kingdom, including its Shia Muslim citizens."[12]

WHAT CAN BE DONE TO HELP THE SAUDIS GAIN MORE RELIGIOUS FREEDOM?

Perhaps the only way religious minorities will be able to exercise their full rights is if the Saudi kingdom falls and is replaced by a secular state. But no one knows if, or when, that might happen. For now, pressing the kingdom for reforms is critical.

These reforms would include freedom of worship for non-Muslims and Shia; an end to arrests for apostasy, blasphemy, and sorcery; the prosecution of clerics who incite violence against religious minorities; repeal of the 2014 Terrorist Act section that treats atheism and blasphemy as forms of terrorism; public education that teaches respect for different religious beliefs; and equality in employment and in the justice system.

Foreign governments and UN bodies must act more forcefully to push for these reforms and support Saudis speaking out for religious freedom. While some of these institutions, including U.S. congressional representatives, have condemned Saudi religious repression and outlined needed reforms, they have done little or nothing to put effective pressure on the government.

This is certainly true of the U.S. government. The U.S. Commission on International Religious Freedom puts out detailed yearly reports on Saudi abuses. According to U.S. law, specifically the 1998 International Religious Freedom Act (IRFA), these abuses against freedom of religion in Saudi Arabia should trigger executive sanctions that could range from canceling cultural activities or official visits, to denying U.S. visas to Saudi officials or halting commercial deals.[13] Shamefully, in 2004 the State Department issued an "indefinite waiver" that has taken the Saudis off the hook.[14] While some hoped that the State Department under President Obama would lift the waiver, this did not happen.

The international community needs to get serious. It must set firm timelines for changes and then implement sanctions if deadlines pass without those transformations being made. Otherwise, Saudi Arabia will continue to be a U.S. ally that denies its inhabitants the most basic right to worship as they please.

CHAPTER 3: BEHEADINGS AND TORTURE IN THE SAUDI "JUSTICE SYSTEM"

Looking at basic freedoms such as free speech, free association, or a fair judicial system, Saudi Arabia flunks on all levels. Freedom House, a U.S. nongovernmental organization that tracks human rights, year after year rates Saudi Arabia as "not free" and gives it the lowest possible score, in a league with countries such as North Korea, Syria, and Sudan.[1]

WHAT ABOUT FREEDOM OF EXPRESSION?

There is almost a total intolerance of dissent, be it political, religious, or ideological. Saudi jails are crowded with those whose only crimes were to speak— or type—freely.

The press is tightly controlled. The Basic Law of Governance, the document that defines the relationship between the rulers and the ruled, says the press must be "civil and polite." In reality, civil and polite means the media must conform to the dictates of the rulers and submit to a severe system of monitoring and control.

The government itself dominates regional print and satellite-television coverage, with members of the royal family owning major stakes in news outlets. Government officials have banned journalists and editors who publish articles deemed offensive to the religious establishment or the ruling authorities. A 2011 royal decree amended the press law to criminalize any criticism of the country's Grand Mufti (the highest religious leader), the Council of Senior Religious Scholars, or government officials. Violations can result in fines and forced closure of media outlets.

The internet has given the public access to an enormous new source of diverse information, and by 2015 there were twelve million internet users in Saudi Arabia. But a 2011 law requires all blogs and websites, or anyone posting news or commentary online, to have a license from the Ministry of Information. The government regularly sweeps the internet, blocking access to websites it deems immoral or politically sensitive. This can range from sites with "atheistic content" to sites that advocate for the right of Saudi women to drive.

One example of the fierce government crackdown on bloggers is the case of Raif Badawi, creator of the blog *Free Saudi Liberals* (https://sites.google.com/site/freesaudiliberals/). Badawi, a young man with three children, wrote with sarcasm and humor about the need for freethinkers in the Arab world. He called for a separation of religion and state, spoke enthusiastically about the Arab Spring, warned against extremism, and advocated for "liberalism." He made no calls for violence; he simply said Saudis should not be hemmed in by religious ideologies or fear but should be "champions in accepting the beliefs of others."

Badawi was arrested in 2012 on charges that included "insulting Islam through electronic channels." He was originally sentenced to death, a sentence that was later commuted to ten years in prison, a thousand lashes, and a fine of over $250,000. The first fifty lashes were administered in January 2015; thanks to the international outcry, the remaining lashes were postponed, but as of April 2016, Badawi was still in prison.[2]

Another example of severe censorship is the case of Wajdi al-Ghazzawi. In February 2014, after launching a TV talk show called *All-Fadfadah* (Relaxed Conversation) that talked about issues like administrative corruption, a court convicted al-Ghazzawi of "harming the nation's image." He was sentenced to twelve years in prison, banned for life from appearing on media outlets, and forbidden to leave the country for twenty years.[3] In another egregious case in March 2016, prominent journalist Alaa Brinji was convicted of "inciting public opinion" and sentenced to five years in prison for tweets that called for human rights, including the right of women to drive.

"It is inconceivable that mere criticism in statements and on social media could land someone in jail for more than a decade, but that's the sad reality in Saudi Arabia," said Sarah Leah Whitson of Human Rights Watch.[4]

In January 2016 the Saudi government took censorship one step further, holding administrators of chat groups responsible for what people in the group are writing. It issued a decree saying that administrators of chat groups on the popular messaging application WhatsApp have to report any irregularities affecting public morals, religious values, or the government. Failure to do so can make them complicit in a cybercrime that can result in a five-year prison term and a fine of up to $800,000. Mahmoud Ramadan, who manages a number of chat groups, asked: "How can I report my friends or relatives for what might only be an ironic comment? If we have to do this, no one will use these applications anymore."[5]

Cultural products from books to movies to art are controlled. Authorities regularly ban books; more than ten thousand copies of books were confiscated at the annual book fair in Riyadh in 2014. Movie theaters were banned in the 1980s to appease conservative clerics. There have been constant rumors that cinemas would reopen, but as of 2016 they remained closed. The first Saudi feature film directed by a woman, entitled *Wadjda*, was presented to great acclaim at the 2012 Cannes Film Festival, but it was impossible to watch the film in a theater in Saudi Arabia. The ban on movie theaters makes little sense since Saudis can watch movies from Hollywood to Bollywood on TV, download movies on the internet, or buy all kinds of movies on DVD. However, the ban remains in place partly because the clerics worry that dark movie theaters make it easier for men and women to mix.

The regime also tries to control the foreign press. It regularly denies foreign reporters entry visas. When reporters are allowed in the country, they are under the thumb of official government "minders" who make it nearly impossible for them to talk freely to ordinary people. If they file stories the government considers hostile, they can get booted out or refused entry the next time they attempt to enter the country. In a recent groundbreaking

2016 PBS *Frontline* documentary called *Saudi Arabia Uncovered*, foreign journalists had to create a fake business in order to gain entry to the country. Once inside, they were approached by government officials with probing questions about their cover, and later their fake online site was hacked. Fearing for their safety, they cut their trip short with virtually no reporting or exploration in the country, and flew home.[6]

Saudi nationals who give interviews to foreign correspondents may also face severe consequences. In 2014, prominent Eastern Province activist Fadhil al-Manasif was sentenced to fifteen years in prison, a fifteen-year ban on travel abroad, and a large fine for charges that included "contact with foreign news organizations to exaggerate the news," and "circulating his phone number to [foreign] news agencies to allow them to call him." The charges stemmed from the assistance al-Manasif provided to international media covering the 2011 protests in the Eastern Province.[7]

Reporters Without Borders ranks Saudi Arabia near the bottom of its global free press index, coming in at 164 out of 180 countries.[8]

WHAT ABOUT FREEDOM OF ASSOCIATION?

All public gatherings, including demonstrations, are prohibited under an order issued by the Interior Ministry in 2011. Those who defy the ban face arrest, prosecution, and imprisonment on charges such as "inciting people against the authorities."

Saudi officials deny holding political prisoners, but in reality, Saudi authorities maintain their iron grip on power through the systematic and ruthless persecution of peaceful activists. According to Amnesty International, "Peaceful human rights activists have been routinely harassed, rounded up like criminals and often ill-treated in detention as the Saudi Arabian authorities go to extreme lengths to hound critics into silent submission."[9] Thousands of activists have disappeared into the black hole of prisons without charges. Saudis are often caught in a revolving door of detention, release, and detention, making it hard to clearly call someone a detainee or to track numbers.

In 2009 a group of eleven courageous human rights activists, reform-minded Islamists, and academics founded the Saudi Civil and Political Rights Association (ACPRA, but better known by its Arabic acronym HASEM). Among its prominent members were economics professor Muhammad Fahad al-Qahtani and professor of comparative literature Abdullah al-Hamid. The group advocated for an elected parliament and legal institutions that would be transparent and accountable. It called for the right of Saudi citizens to have basic freedoms of expression and assembly, and campaigned for the release or fair trial of long-term political detainees.

One of the most interesting aspects of HASEM, and one that the Saudi government probably found particularly threatening, was that it brought together non-Islamists with Islamists whose reinterpretation of Islamic texts supported democracy, civil society, and human rights.

MEDEA BENJAMIN

During the next few years, the Saudi authorities began targeting the founders, one by one, in a brutal campaign to silence them and break up the association. By 2014, three of the founders were serving prison terms of up to fifteen years, three were awaiting trial, three more were facing a retrial, and two others were detained without trial. Some members were tortured while in detention; others were held incommunicado and in solitary confinement for several months. They were charged with Orwellian crimes under the anti-terrorism laws such as "disobeying the ruler," "undermining the integrity of the state," and "inciting public opinion against the authorities." The government dissolved the group in 2013 and seized its assets for the crime of "failing to obtain a license"—a license that the government had refused to grant.[10]

Even the lawyers who defend brave human rights activists are in danger. The country's terrorism court convicted human rights lawyer Waleed Abu al-Khair to a fifteen-year prison sentence in 2014 for criticizing human rights abuses and for defending peaceful activists, including jailed blogger Raif Badawi. Abu al-Khair's wife, Samar Badawi, has faced a ban on travel abroad, apparently due to her advocacy on behalf of her husband at the UN Human Rights Council in 2014.

In 2003 King Fahd authorized the formation of the National Society for Human Rights and in 2005 it formally established the Human Rights Commission, whose president sits on the Council of Ministers. These two institutions have made efforts to improve human rights, but their connection to the government severely limits their scope of action.

Saudis have long struggled for the right to form their own nongovernment associations, be they charity groups, professional associations, trade unions, or human rights groups. Even nonpolitical groups like the Cancer Foundation or the Diabetes Association had to wait years for government approval. The government has routinely refused to license political or human rights groups, leaving their members vulnerable to prosecution for participating in unregistered organizations.

In December 2015, for the first time in the kingdom's history, the government issued a new law providing a legal framework for nongovernmental organizations (NGOs). How this law will be implemented and whether it will allow the creation of a more open civil society remains to be seen.[11]

There are no labor unions in the country and no laws protect workers' rights to form independent labor unions, bargain collectively, or engage in strikes. Workers who attempt to engage in union activity are subject to dismissal or imprisonment. The government allows labor committees in workplaces of over one hundred employees, but keeps tight control of them and does not allow any of the millions of migrant workers to join. The Ministry of Labor approves the committee members and authorizes employer representatives to attend the meetings, and the ministry can dissolve the committees at any time if they are deemed to "threaten public security."

When the International Trade Union Confederation launched its 2015 Global Rights Index detailing the ten worst countries for workers' rights in the world, Saudi Arabia was one of the ten.[12]

HOW FAIR IS THE JUDICIARY?

As in many Islamic nations, Saudi Arabia's legal system is based on judges, who are clerics, interpreting Sharia law. The particular Saudi version, however, is one of the strictest interpretations of Islamic law in the modern age. Educated in state-run seminaries, judges learn how to interpret centuries-old judicial texts and apply them in court. In matters not clearly defined in the Quran or the *hudud* (a section of Sharia law that deals with serious crimes), they are supposed to consider precedents set by other judges and laws implemented by the government, but they have vast discretion. In the absence of a written penal code or narrowly worded regulations, judges and prosecutors are free to apply rules inconsistently and criminalize a wide range of offenses under broad, catch-all charges, such as "breaking allegiance with the ruler" or "trying to distort the reputation of the kingdom."

Suspects are sometimes unaware of the crime they are charged with and not given access to supporting evidence, even after trial sessions have begun. Authorities generally do not allow lawyers to assist suspects during interrogation, and often impede them from examining witnesses and presenting evidence at trial.

Access to prisoners by independent human rights and legal organizations is also strictly limited. The government denies access to Amnesty International and has even taken punitive action against activists and family members of victims who contact the organization.

In 2014, responding to new terrorist attacks by the Islamic State inside Saudi territory, the government instituted a sweeping new "anti-terrorism" law (called the Penal Law for Crimes of Terrorism and Its Financing). The law goes far beyond dealing with violent attacks; it treats virtually all dissident thought or free expression as acts of terrorism. Terrorist acts include "calling for atheist thought," "contacting any groups or individuals opposed to the Kingdom," "seeking to disrupt national unity" by calling for protests, and "harming other states and their leaders."

This far-reaching law grants extensive powers to the interior minister that undermine what little due process existed in Saudi law. It empowers the minister to order arrests of terrorism suspects without going through the public prosecutor, and grants him access to the suspect's private banking and communications information, all without judicial oversight. It authorizes the Specialized Criminal Court to hear witnesses and experts without the presence of the defendant or the defendant's lawyer. Two days after the terrorism law took effect, King Abdullah issued Royal Decree 44, making "participating in hostilities outside the kingdom" a crime punishable by a prison term of three to twenty years. The rationale was to stop Saudis from joining groups like Al Qaeda or the Islamic State, but the decree was so sweeping that it could include support for a foreign political party.

"King Abdullah was once considered a cautious reformer but the new terrorism law could wipe out a decade of the most modest progress," said Joe Stork, Deputy Middle East Director at Human Rights Watch. "Instead of loosening the reins on Saudi society, the king is empowering criminal justice authorities to arrest and try peaceful activists along with suspected terrorists."[13]

When you add together the strict Wahhabi interpretation of Islamic law, the lack of checks and balances, the wide breadth of judges' discretion, and the sweeping anti terrorism laws, the result is a judicial system rife with abuse.

HOW COMMON IS THE USE OF TORTURE?

Torture is banned by law, but according to former detainees and human rights advocates, it is widespread and administered with impunity by police and prison officials. Courts have convicted defendants—and even sentenced them to death solely on the basis of pretrial "confessions" extracted under torture.

Sandy Mitchell, a British man held in a Saudi jail between 2000 and 2003 for a murder he did not commit, wrote a book about his harrowing experience. He was tortured repeatedly until he confessed, forced to read his confession on television, tortured again so he wouldn't recant, and then sentenced to death after a ten-minute secret trial. "All during the night I would be tortured. They punched, kicked and spat at me, and later hit me with sticks. They used an axe handle to beat the soles of my feet. I would have confessed to anything to stop the pain," he said.[14]

A common punishment that inflicts tremendous pain is flogging, which is usually carried out in public squares for all to witness. Human rights defender Mikhlif bin Daham al-Shammari was sentenced to two hundred lashes, as well as a prison term, for advocating reforms. In 2014, Ruth Cosrojas, a Filipino domestic worker, was sentenced to eighteen months' imprisonment and 150 lashes after an unfair trial where she was convicted of organizing the sale of sex. The UN High Commissioner for Human Rights, Zeid Ra'ad Al Hussein, said: "Flogging is, in my view, at the very least, a form of cruel and inhuman punishment. Such punishment is prohibited under international human rights law, in particular the Convention against Torture, which Saudi Arabia has ratified."[15]

Saudi Arabia also punishes people by amputating their limbs, although this has fortunately become rare. Executioner Muhammad Saad al-Beshi gave a hauntingly frank interview in 2003 where he said that for amputations, he uses a special knife that his children help him sharpen. "When I cut off a hand, I cut it from the joint. If it is a leg, the authorities specify where it is to be taken off, so I follow that."[16] In 2005, the Saudi courts ordered that Indian citizen Puthan Veettil Abd ul-Latif Noushad have his right eye gouged out for participating in a fight that had left a Saudi citizen with a wounded eye. In 2013, a Yemeni man convicted of robbery had his right hand cut off.

HOW OFTEN DO THEY USE THE DEATH PENALTY?

Saudi Arabia generally ranks third in the world for executions, behind China and Iran. The death penalty is disproportionately meted out to poor Saudis and foreigners from poor countries. Nearly half those executed between 1985 and 2015 were

MEDEA BENJAMIN

foreigners, in part because they don't have influential figures to intervene on their behalf, are victims of a discriminatory court system, and don't understand Arabic.

The majority of death penalty sentences are for nonviolent offenses. Of the 171 prisoners death row as of 2015, 72 percent were convicted of nonviolent crimes, especially drug offenses.[17] Among those convicted for drugs might be hardcore heroin smugglers coming from Pakistan, but they are more likely to be poor migrants caught with hash. Meanwhile, Saudi princes are regularly caught overseas smuggling enormous quantities of drugs but are usually allowed to return home, scot-free.

In 1996, the UN Special Rapporteur on Extrajudicial, Summary or Arbitrary Executions said the death penalty should be eliminated for drug-related offenses.

Other crimes punishable by death are banditry, murder, pedophilia, homosexuality, treason, blasphemy (insulting God, the Prophet, or Islam), and apostasy (renouncing Islam). All sexual activity outside marriage, including same-sex activity, is criminalized, and the death penalty can be applied in certain circumstances.

Another crime punishable by death is sorcery, which means the use of magical powers obtained through evil spirits. (While death for sorcery is unthinkable in most of the world today, thousands were executed for witchcraft in Europe and the American colonies in past centuries.) In 2014, the Saudi Ministry of Justice announced that prosecutors had filed 191 cases of alleged sorcery between November 2013 and May 2014, including some against foreign domestic workers.

Examples of beheadings for sorcery include Muree bin Issa al-Asiri, who was found in possession of talismans and was executed in the southern Najran province in June 2012; a Saudi woman, Amina bin Salem Nasser, convicted of practicing sorcery and witchcraft in December 2011 in the northern province of Jawf; and a Sudanese man, Abdul Moustafa al-Fakki, who was executed for sorcery in a car park in Medina in September 2011.

"Any execution is appalling, but executions for crimes such as drug smuggling or sorcery that result in no loss of life are particularly egregious," said Sarah Leah Whitson, Middle East and North Africa Director of Human Rights Watch. "There is simply no excuse for Saudi Arabia's continued use of the death penalty, especially for these types of crimes."[18]

Those sentenced to death have the right to seek pardon or commutation of their sentence from the king. When there is a public outcry, the king may step in and grant a pardon, but this is totally unpredictable and politically motivated.

Executions are usually carried out by public beheading, more rarely by firing squad or by stoning. Saudi Arabia, Iran, North Korea, and Somalia are the only countries that still execute people in public. If the prisoner is in the capital city, the beheading—with the swift blow of a sword—is likely carried out in Deera Square, also known by the macabre nickname Chop Chop Square. The grisly public spectacle is supposed to act as a deterrent to others. Even more gruesome is the sentence of crucifixion, which means the prisoner is first beheaded, then the body is tied to a pole, with the detached head floating above the body. The corpse might be kept in that position for up to four days, serving as a grotesque warning to others.

Human rights advocates have noted that these sorts of punishments resemble those used by the Islamic State, an enemy of both Saudi Arabia and the United States. "Imagine how shocking and horrifying it would be if every Saudi beheading was posted on YouTube?" Whitson says. "Washington, and others in the anti-ISIS coalition, should think long and hard about the example their ally is setting."[19]

In 2015, the number of executions reached a twenty-year high of 158 people; over seventy of them were foreign nationals. The last person executed was Abdulatif Zapanta, a Filipino who worked as a tile layer and killed his Sudanese landlord in a violent dispute over rent money. He claimed self-defense and would have been granted a reprieve if he paid a fine of about $1 million. He was beheaded when he was unable to raise the money.[20]

The government started out the year 2016 with a mass execution of forty-seven prisoners on January 2. One of those killed, prominent Shia cleric Nimr al-Nimr, drew global attention and outrage. He was killed along with three other Shia Muslims from the Eastern Province.

Sheikh al-Nimr was a vociferous critic of the regime and the ongoing discrimination against the Shia minority, but he never advocated or was involved in violence. He became particularly controversial in 2012 in the aftermath of a new round of protests spawned in large part by the Arab Spring. Security forces violently arrested the fifty-three-year-old cleric in July 2012, shooting him multiple times. During his detention, the authorities denied him access to adequate medical care, failing to properly treat his paralyzed right leg or remove a bullet from his body. After holding him for months without charge, he was brought to trial before the Specialized Criminal Court, the kingdom's anti-terrorism tribunal.

The cleric's trial was grossly unfair. The judge prevented him from adequately preparing his defense, meeting with his lawyer, or cross-examining witnesses. In October 2014, he was sentenced to death on a number of broad charges, including "disobeying and breaking allegiance to the ruler," "calling to overthrow the regime," "calling for demonstrations," and "inciting sectarian strife."

The sheikh's execution led to protests all over the globe, especially in countries with a large Shia population. In Iran, protesters burned the Saudi Embassy, and the Saudis reacted by cutting off relations with Iran.

In 2016 three young Shia prisoners were still on death row, awaiting imminent execution. Ali al-Nimr (the sheikh's nephew), Dawood al-Marhoon, and Abdullah al-Zaher were all arrested for participating in peaceful protests and were all juveniles (fifteen to seventeen years old) at the time of their arrest. They were sentenced to death after trials based on "confessions" extracted under torture. Dawood al-Marhoon was tortured so badly that he signed a blank piece of paper; his tormentors later filled in the "confession" without even bothering to show it to him. Ali al-Nimr was sentenced not only to execution, but also to crucifixion.[21]

Saudi law prohibits the execution of minors, so the government holds juveniles until they are over eighteen and then beheads them. These three prisoners await their fate while international human rights advocates are campaigning to save their lives. A CODEPINK video calling for the release of Ali al-Nimr got over one million views. "The only thing keeping these young men alive is international attention," said attorney Julianne Hill with the UK-based group Reprieve.[22]

With forty-seven executions on January 2, 2016, alone, the number of yearly executions will most likely continue to rise. It is difficult to pinpoint a cause for the increase. Theories range from changes in the judicial system that expedite sentencing to a more severe king and interior minister to the overall instability in the region.

IS THERE A GAY COMMUNITY AND DO GAY PEOPLE HAVE ANY RIGHTS?

The Saudi attitude toward homosexuality is fraught with contradictions. Saudi Arabia is one of ten countries in the world where homosexuality can be punished by death. A married man engaging in sodomy, or any non-Muslim man who commits sodomy with a Muslim, can be executed. Other possible punishments for homosexuality include chemical castration (via injection or tablets), although the most common punishment is imprisonment and fines.

At the same time, however, there are active gay communities for men in cosmopolitan cities like Jeddah and Riyadh. Gay men connect in cafes, in schools, in the streets, and on the internet. If they keep their liaisons discreet, the religious police usually leave them alone.

One reason for this surprising tolerance is that same-gender sex is actually quite common, even among people who are heterosexual. One young anonymous Saudi told me, "Homosexual acts are actually common because of the unique constraints Saudi society places on interactions between men and women. In all-boys' schools, boys fulfill their sexual desires with other boys; girls do, too. But we don't necessarily consider it homosexuality because it often doesn't happen out of choice but out of the extreme gender separation."[23] A young woman quoted in an *Atlantic* article entitled "The Kingdom in the Closet" said that many young people had lesbian or gay sex because it was so much easier, given all the restrictions on men and women interacting before marriage. "They're not really homosexual," she said. "They're like cell mates in prison."[24]

Some young members of the Saudi royal family are known for their outrageous sexual behavior in their jaunts overseas. A Saudi prince on vacation in Beverly Hills, supposedly high on cocaine, was arrested for forcing himself on three female workers and then making them watch as a man "performed a sexual act on him." He never went to jail, either in the United States or back home.[25]

As in every other aspect of society, the wealthier, Sunni, Saudi nationals are granted much greater leniency. While there may be a degree of tolerance for wealthy princes and the more privileged sectors of society, the less privileged—including migrant workers and the Shiite minority—face much graver repercussions.

In November 2015, a court in Saudi Arabia's eastern port city of Dammam sentenced a man to three years in prison and a fine of $26,000 for allegedly engaging in "immoral acts" of homosexuality. In July 2014, a twenty-four-year-old man in the city of Medina was sentenced to three years in jail and 450 lashes after being entrapped in a Facebook ploy by the religious police. The court found him guilty of "promoting the vice and practice of homosexuality."[26] In 2011, a British man, Stephen Comiskey, was arrested and beaten by Saudi religious police when they discovered he was gay, and a Filipino man spent nine months in prison and got 200 lashes for attending a party featuring a drag show.

When the United Nations was setting its Sustainable Development Goals in 2015, Saudi representatives successfully lobbied for the UN to remove gay rights from the goals because such rights, they argued, run counter to Islamic law.

WHAT ARE THE PROSPECTS FOR REFORM?

Thanks to the internet, Saudi Arabia's abysmal human rights record has come under unprecedented international scrutiny. Videos of beheadings and other outrageous treatment have gone viral and produced outrage. Groups such as Human Rights Watch and Amnesty International have helped publicize numerous cases, from the public flogging of bloggers to the beheading of migrant women.

Public pressure has forced some Western governments to bring up these issues with their Saudi counterparts, but there have been no international sanctions and few public condemnations.

In 2014, seventy members of the U.S. Congress signed a letter to President Obama urging him to confront Saudi leaders on human rights abuses. During Obama's 2014 visit to Saudi Arabia, Amnesty International urged the president to select a female Secret Service officer as his driver to highlight the ban on Saudi women driving. He declined.

In an interview with CNN's Fareed Zakaria in January 2015, after he returned from the funeral of King Abdullah, President Obama reasoned, "Sometimes we have to balance our need to speak to them about human rights issues with immediate concerns that we have in terms of countering terrorism or dealing with regional stability."[27]

That "balance," in all its hypocrisy, was evident when Saudi Arabia was granted a seat on the UN Human Rights Council in 2013. Classified UK diplomatic files passed to WikiLeaks two years later reveal that a secret vote-trading deal was made by Britain and Saudi Arabia to ensure both countries were elected to the council.[28] Adding insult to injury, in 2015, the Saudi ambassador to the UN in Geneva was elected Chair of the UN Human Rights Council panel that appoints independent experts. UN Watch executive director Hillel Neuer said, "It is scandalous that the UN chose a country that has beheaded more people this year than ISIS to be head of a key human rights panel. Petro-dollars and politics have trumped human rights."[29]

Amnesty International's Said Boumedouha echoed the views of many human rights activists when he said, "Without international condemnation and concrete pressure on the authorities, Saudi Arabia will continue to flagrantly violate the most basic human rights principles unchecked."[30]

CHAPTER 4: THE STRUGGLE OF SAUDI WOMEN FOR EQUAL RIGHTS

The image foreigners often have of Saudi women is a shapeless figure cloaked in black, some with only their eyes showing through veils. This is the superficial image. But what is the real status of women in this patriarchal society?

WHAT IS THE MALE GUARDIANSHIP POLICY?

While there have been major gains for Saudi women in the past decades due to campaigns by women themselves and reforms implemented by the late King Abdullah, Saudi Arabia remains the most gender-segregated nation in the world. The discriminatory male guardianship system persists despite government pledges to abolish it. Under this system, a woman, no matter her age, is treated as a minor and must live under the supervision of a *wali*, or guardian. This is a legally recognized male—her father, husband, uncle, or some other male relative (even her son)—who must grant formal permission for most of the significant issues affecting her life. Some refer to this system as a form of gender apartheid.

Women are not allowed to marry, obtain a passport, or travel without the permission of their guardians. Enrollment in education requires a guardian's approval, although some universities are no longer requiring this. Employers often require male guardians to approve the hiring of females.

In May 2016 a new reform touted in the international media made it compulsory that a married woman's guardian give her a copy of her marriage certificate so she is aware of the conditions of the marriage. Previously, only men were allowed to have a copy of the certificate.

Unlike men, women do not have a unilateral right to divorce. A wife can obtain a divorce only if she pays back her dowry or can prove in court that her husband has harmed her; a man can divorce his wife unilaterally, without any legal justification.

Women also face discrimination when it comes to child custody. A Saudi woman may keep her children until they reach the age of seven for girls and nine for boys. Custody of children over these ages is generally awarded to the father. In rare cases where women are granted physical custody, fathers retain legal custody, meaning that most transactions on behalf of the children require the father's consent. Foreign women married to Saudi nationals also suffer discrimination in custody and divorce matters.

Citizenship is transferred to children through their father, so a child born to an unwed mother is not legally affiliated with the father and is therefore "stateless." Also, the government does not automatically grant Saudi citizenship to the children of Saudi women if their fathers are not Saudi. Sons can apply for citizenship but the decision is at the discretion of the Interior Minister. Daughters of Saudi mothers and non-Saudi fathers are not granted citizenship unless they marry a Saudi husband and give birth to a child. In September 2015, the Supreme Judicial Council granted women with custody of their children the right to handle all their affairs, but they still need permission from the children's father to travel outside the country.

In certain types of cases in court, female testimony is worth half as much as male testimony. If a woman is in prison or in a rehabilitation center, she cannot be released to anyone but her guardian; if the guardian refuses to accept the woman, as often happens, she remains imprisoned.

Some hospitals require the male guardian's approval for certain medical procedures. Women are not allowed to expose their body to a male healthcare worker unless it is a medical emergency. In 2015, a member of the Senior Council of Scholars, the highest state body for the interpretation of Islamic law, issued a *fatwa* stating that women are not allowed to visit a male doctor without their male guardians. But this is not the law and in practice, many women attend healthcare facilities without guardians.

Saudi blogger Eman al-Nafjan, complaining about the devastating effects of the male guardianship system, poses the dilemma of a friend being abused by her father. "If I report the situation to the police and they take it seriously enough to go to my friend's house, her father—as her legal guardian—could simply dismiss them at the door. Even if my friend gathers the courage to go to the police station herself, she is more likely to be sent to prison than her father is. Her charge would be disobeying her father."[1]

The real problem, explained Saudi journalist Ebtihal Mubarak, is the tremendous authority this system gives to the male figure. "It's not that Saudi men hate women, but having so much power can bring out the monster in men."[2]

"Some women are lucky and their guardians allow them the freedom to travel, to get an education, to work, or to marry the person they choose, but many Saudi women are not that lucky," wrote blogger Suzie Khalil. "This guardianship system basically means that Saudi women are totally powerless over their own lives and destinies unless their male guardian allows them that power."[3]

DO WOMEN HAVE ACCESS TO EDUCATION?

In the past few decades, there has been a huge opening in women's access to education. Very few girls went to school before 1960, when the first state-run girls' school was opened. In 2004, a royal decree made primary education compulsory for all children—male and female--between the ages of six and fifteen. Primary and secondary education became free and accessible, even in rural areas. By 2012, the literacy rate for girls was 97 percent.[4]

The number of Saudi women graduating from university has grown tremendously since the 1960s, when the first women's colleges were created. By 2010 there were over three hundred women's colleges and the majority of college graduates were women.[5]

Schools, however, are separate for males and females from elementary school to postgraduate degrees (with the sole exception of King Abdullah University of Science and Technology, where the school is mixed but classes are still segregated). The norm is that females teach females and males teach males, but due to a shortage of male teachers, some private schools are allowed to let women teach all-boys classes until third grade.

Women have had to fight not only for the right to go to school, but also for quality education. Conservative clerics believed that allowing girls to study at public schools would expose them to the corrupting values of Western culture and cause them to reject their "proper role"—staying home and raising children. So they insisted that girls' schools be placed under the Department of Religious Guidance and that girls, unlike boys, should be taught a narrow range of subjects, mostly Islamic studies, Arabic language, basic math, and housekeeping.

As more and more women became educated, they challenged the clerics and demanded more options. Ironically, two tragedies helped open new doors. The 9/11 attacks in the United States put Saudi Arabia under greater international scrutiny for the suppression of women's rights. So did a 2002 fire in an elementary girls' school that killed fifteen students because the religious police stopped them from escaping when they weren't "properly dressed."

With growing opposition to the religious control of girl's education, in 2002 girls' schools were finally taken away from the

Department of Religious Guidance and put under the Ministry of Education, which had always been in charge of boys' education.

But women were still barred from certain professions, such as engineering and law. It was not until 2008 that the first women graduated from law school, and in 2013, the first four women received their legal licenses to practice law in court-rooms and before the Saudi judiciary.[6] Women are still not allowed to be judges.

In 2006 King Abdullah stipulated that girls and boys should have the same curriculum, but this has not been fully imple-mented. Another major breakthrough was the establishment of King Abdullah's scholarships, offering funds for students—male and female—to attend universities around the world and giving women the right to major in the same fields as men. As of 2014, more than thirty-five thousand Saudi women were enrolled in foreign undergraduate and graduate programs, and over half were studying in the United States.[7] Even then, however, a male guardian must approve the scholarship and is formally required to travel with her to the country where she chooses to study in order for the scholarship to be valid.

CAN SAUDI WOMEN PLAY SPORTS?

For decades there has been a ban on sports for girls. In 2013, the ban was lifted for private schools, as long as the girls wear "decent clothing" and are supervised by female instructors. In 2014, the Shura Council recommended that the ban be lifted for public schools as well, but bringing PE classes to the public schools has been slow in coming.

According to Human Rights Watch, Saudi Arabia is the only country in the world with a policy of denying access to physical education in government-run schools. Saudi Arabia also bars females from attending public sporting events as spectators (as does Iran).

The ban on sports for women is not only an act of gender discrimination; it violates the right of women to lead healthy lives. The report *Killing Them Softly* by the Institute for Gulf Affairs claims that the sedentary lifestyle of Saudi women has led to high levels of obesity, heart disease, high blood pressure, Type 2 diabetes, vitamin D deficiency, osteoporosis, and depression, among other ailments.[8]

It was not until 2013 that Saudi women were first allowed to ride bicycles, although only around parks and other "recreational areas." The women must be dressed in their abayas and be accompanied by a male relative.

Saudi officials banned Saudi women from participating in the Olympics because they deemed that the attire used in most competitive Olympic sports was not modest. The kingdom came under intense international pressure for this ban. In 2012, they allowed two Saudi women to compete under the Saudi flag, one in track and one in judo, but both women lived outside the country.

A campaign called No Women No Play has been pressing the International Olympic Committee to suspend Saudi Arabia because of its discrimination against female athletes. The group is also targeting FIFA, the International Federation of Association Football. Saudi Arabia is a member of FIFA, and has had a national men's soccer team for years, but no women's soccer team. FIFA statutes say that gender discrimination is strictly prohibited, so No Women No Play says FIFA should suspend or expel Saudi Arabia until it complies with FIFA's standards.

A few private women's health clubs and gyms have opened in recent years. A group called Jeddah United Sports Company, founded in 2006, got a license from the Ministry of Commerce to train women athletes in Jeddah (the Ministry of Sports refused to license them) and has expanded to several cities. These private initiatives are promising openings, although they are nowhere near what is needed to ensure that Saudi's ten million women and girls have an opportunity to develop a love for sports and exercise. But at least in this area of discrimination, there is a lot of female energy to burst through the obstacles in their path.

WHAT WORK OPTIONS ARE OPEN FOR WOMEN?

Saudi women make up 60 percent of the nation's college students but, according to the World Bank, in 2014 they made up only 20 percent of the labor force, much lower than in neighboring countries.[9] And while unemployment among Saudi males was about 6 percent in 2015, among females it was 33 percent.[10] Of the people receiving unemployment benefits in 2012, over 80 percent were women.[11]

Women also have limited job options. Yes, there are women who are architects, scientists, and even pilots, but most women are educated and then funneled into jobs that, according to government policy, "suit her nature, which are education and healthcare": 85 percent of employed Saudi women work in education and 6 percent in public health.[12] Women with college degrees and even PhDs have a hard time finding jobs; the greatest sector of unemployed is female college graduates.

It is possible to find women who own stores, restaurants, beauty salons, and even their own consulting firms, but women entrepreneurs are rare. In fact, 95 percent of working women are employed in the public sector.

Concerned about unemployment, especially after the Arab Spring uprisings that swept the region in 2011, the government started the "Saudization program" to pressure businesses to hire Saudis over foreign workers (who are lower paid and have far fewer rights). And a 2016 plan called Saudi Vision 2030, designed to reduce Saudi reliance on oil, included a goal to increase women's participation in the workforce to 30 percent by 2030.

This government pressure has opened doors to women in sectors that can accommodate the kingdom's strict rules on gender segregation. Some companies constructed partitions to create separate workspaces for women. Some offer transportation stipends for female employees, since they are not allowed to drive. Others have been experimenting with virtual offices, allowing women to work from home.

The government sponsors trainings to help women enter the workforce. For many women, it is the first time they interact with men outside their immediate families.

The backlash from conservatives has caused some companies to retreat. When a supermarket chain first hired female cashiers, a prominent cleric called for a boycott of the stores; the company caved in and let the women go.

In 2006 the government passed a law requiring that stores catering exclusively to women hire female salespeople. (Women had previously been forced to buy everything, including intimate female products, from men.) But even then, it took intensive lobbying, a social media campaign, and a 2011 royal decree to get the law enforced, starting with lingerie and cosmetics stores, then extending to all women's department stores. There are now women working in retail across the country, but only in segregated spaces and selling to women.

The government enforces sex segregation in virtually all workplaces except hospitals, and fines companies that fail to comply. Segregation not only applies to the workforce, but also the clients. If you are thinking of sipping a latte at a front table in a Riyadh Starbucks, and you are a woman, think again. In food outlets, all lines, counters, and eating areas are separated to keep unrelated men and women apart. Restaurants and cafes have one section for "singles," meaning men, and one for "families," meaning women, children, and close male relatives like husbands. The men's section is usually at the front, while women and families usually sit in a partitioned area at the back, shielded from public view.

Unlawful mixing can lead to fines for the institution and criminal charges against the violators (with women typically facing harsher punishment than men). The majority of public buildings have separate entrances for men and women; some even ban women from entering.

WHAT IS THE DRESS CODE FOR WOMEN?

While all versions of Islam suggest a woman should dress modestly, Saudi Arabia is one of the only Muslim-majority countries that legally imposes a dress code (Iran is another, although it is less severe).

By law, in public places women must cover their everyday clothing with an abaya. The traditional abaya is a thick, opaque, and loose-fitting cloak that conceals the shape of women's bodies. It covers all but their hands and face, and it is usually used along with the *hijab*, or headscarf. While their faces need not be covered, some women opt for wearing a *niqab*, which is a face veil that covers everything except the eyes.

While men can choose to wear jeans, suits, or the white Arabian robes called *thobes*, women past adolescence must wear abayas.

In public, women may only take off their abayas inside hospitals, certain gated residential areas for foreigners, and in women-only facilities. One of the fanciest shopping malls in Riyadh, for example, contains a whole floor strictly for women.

Wealthy woman have a lot more freedom when it comes to dress because the religious police usually stay away from fancy

MEDEA BENJAMIN

restaurants, hotels, and neighborhoods. Wealthy women (and foreigners) can even go to private beaches that are off-limits to the religious police, where they can swim in bikinis instead of burqinis (the abaya like swimwear most Saudi women must wear).

Saudi women take immense pride in their appearance and enjoy trendy clothing. At home with relatives and in all-female settings, women dress as they please. The accessory industry is thriving in Saudi, as women use shoes, handbags, sunglasses, and jewelry to express their individualism. In regions like the more liberal western coastal city of Jeddah, the dress code is less strict and women can choose from a range of brightly colored, embroidered, and even tightly fitting abayas that are worn open to expose the clothing beneath.

A rare 2014 survey about women's dress found conservative attitudes among both Saudi men and women. While 47 percent of people surveyed said women should be free to wear what they choose, 66 percent thought it was more appropriate if women wore the niqab.[13]

The dress code is enforced by zealous volunteers and the religious police. A video outside a Riyadh mall of the religious police beating a woman who refused to cover her face went viral, dividing online commenters between supporters and critics of the kingdom's religious police. The Ministry of Labor also passed a regulation in 2015 to fine female workers caught violating the dress code at their workplace.

Some women insist that the dress code is not a major issue. "What is important to Saudi women is not what they wear, but the continued development of their minds, the acquisition of useful skills, and their integration in a productive way into the progress that Saudi Arabia has made," reads an article about the growing role of professional women in Saudi society.[14]

Others disagree, especially young women and women who have lived overseas. "If the government will not even give us the freedom to choose what we wear, do you think they will respect our decisions regarding anything else?" asked a young Saudi woman studying in the United States.[15]

WHY CAN'T SAUDI WOMEN DRIVE?

Saudi Arabia remains the only country in the world where women are not allowed to drive. There is no specific law prohibiting women from driving, but the Interior Ministry and the police enforce a ban. The only places where women can get away with driving are in rural areas, in gated communities, and inside the compounds of the oil company Aramco.

One reason used to justify the ban is personal safety, implying that women are safer with men behind the wheel. Others insist that the ban protects women from being attacked if they are out alone, and women do indeed worry that when they finally start driving, they might be attacked by fanatics who think women shouldn't drive. A rather humorous excuse to keep women from driving came from a sheikh who issued a fatwa in 2013 saying that women can't drive because driving would harm their ovaries and reproductive systems.[16]

MEDEA BENJAMIN

"I find these excuses insulting and condescending," says Suzie Khalil, an American married to a Saudi. "Saudi Arabia ranks among the world's worst countries for traffic fatalities. That's what happens when only men are allowed to drive. Despite the fact that I have driven safely in the United States since I was fifteen (that's almost forty years!), I am not allowed behind the wheel in Saudi Arabia simply because I don't have a penis."[17]

The ban on driving, along with the general lack of reliable and safe public transportation, has a terrible impact on women who can't afford their own drivers. The bustling cities, crowded with speeding cars and trucks, can be a hazard for women walking or trying to catch a taxi. For women who want to work or who must work to provide for their families, their immobility can make it impossible to hold down a job. Without a job, most women can't afford to hire a personal driver. If a woman has a job, the bulk of her salary might go to paying her driver.

A Saudi woman from Jeddah explained how expensive it is for a family to hire a driver. Drivers are foreign men who usually live in the employer's home. In addition to the salary, the employer has to pay fees for recruiting agencies, visas, airfare, medical check-ups, driver's licenses, traffic tickets, extra living quarters, furniture, insurance, meals, medical bills, medicine, and extra use of water and electricity. "What a huge financial burden for a country with a shrinking middle class, and with minimum wages not much higher than that paid to a driver brought in from a developing country, many of whom have never driven a car before coming to work in Saudi Arabia," she remarks.

She also questions the logic of a deeply conservative society where a foreign man—a stranger—is brought to live in a family's home simply to drive the women.[18]

For decades Saudi women have been calling for lifting the ban on driving. In 1990, a protest was organized by Aisha Almana. Almana is a Saudi woman who had studied in the United States where, she said, she recognized that she was "a human being equal to anyone else. I am a free soul, and I am my own driver."[19] Almana and forty-six other women piled into fourteen cars and drove around Riyadh in a convoy, snaking through the busiest part of the city. On their second lap, they were arrested and thrown in jail. Their passports were confiscated, those with government jobs were fired, and they were denounced in mosques across the country. Since they were from prestigious families, they were released, their jobs eventually reinstated, and their passports returned.

In 2007 women unsuccessfully petitioned King Abdullah for the right to drive, and a 2008 video of activist Wajeha al-Huwaider driving received international attention. In 2011, about seventy women openly challenged the law by driving and a similar protest was organized in 2013. Three days before the targeted date, the Interior Ministry warned that "women in Saudi are banned from driving and laws will be applied against violators." Despite the warning and the police roadblocks set up to catch women drivers, twelve brave women filmed themselves driving, then posted the videos online. Some of the women were imprisoned, fined, suspended from their jobs, banned from traveling, and even threatened with terrorism charges for public incitement.

Aziza al-Yousef, one of the organizers of a 2013 driving campaign, said defiantly, "We are sick and tired of waiting to be given our rights. It's about time for us to take them." She was arrested for driving and only released when her husband bailed her out and pledged that she would not drive again. Again in 2015, two women activists were arrested for driving.[20]

A YouTube video by Saudi comedian Hisham Fageeh satirizing the ban by rewording the Bob Marley song "No Woman No Cry" as "No Woman No Drive" was an instant hit, getting seven million views in one week.[21]

Saudi women are still waiting, however, for the petition or protest or satire that will be the tipping point, forcing the government to finally grant them this most basic of rights.

HOW MANY WIVES CAN MEN HAVE?

In accordance with Sharia law, polygamous marriages are legal in Saudi Arabia. Saudi men may have up to four wives if they treat them all equally. But it that really feasible? While some Saudi women say yes, others complain that when men remarry, they forget about their first wives and children, and even stop supporting them financially.[22]

Few polygamous families in Saudi Arabia live under one roof. Generally, each wife will have her own home. Men used to want the prestige of several wives and many children; nowadays, the emotional and financial demands are so stressful that a 2015 study by the Asian Pacific Society of Cardiology found that men who practiced polygamy are four times more likely to have heart disease than men with a single partner.[23]

With the rising cost of living and increased resistance from young women, the practice has declined significantly. Polygamy in Saudi today is more common among the very wealthy and rural/tribal communities.

Ironically, the late King Abdullah, praised for being an advocate for women's rights, had way more than four wives. He had somewhere between thirty and forty wives (but always only four at a time), and four of his daughters have been imprisoned in Jeddah for years for disobeying him.

IS THERE A MINIMUM AGE FOR MARRIAGE?

Saudi Arabia and Yemen are the only Arab countries that do not have laws setting a minimum age for marriage. While the average age for Saudi women to marry is a healthy twenty-five, child brides are still acceptable, especially among poor, rural families where girls may be married off to richer, older men.

A push by human rights activists and the Saudi justice ministry to raise the legal age of marriage to fifteen was crushed after the Grand Mufti, Sheikh Abdul-Aziz ibn Al ash-Sheikh, ruled that Islam allows men to marry child brides.[24] The practice is based on Sharia precepts that associate maturity with puberty, which could start as early as nine.

The lives of countless young girls have been destroyed by their being married off when they were children. The Saudi Human Rights Commission, for example, stepped in to help a twelve-year-old girl get a divorce from her abusive eighty-year-old husband.

CAN WOMEN VOTE, RUN FOR OFFICE, AND HOLD POSITIONS OF POWER?

There are very few women in powerful government positions. In 2009 Norah Al Faiz was appointed by King Abdullah to a ministerial post as Deputy Education Minister for Female Education. This was the highest position, to date, for a woman to hold. Unfortunately, her tenure was marked by controversies that ranged from whether she had to wear a veil and how to work with male subordinates to her efforts to introduce physical education in girls' schools. When King Salman came to power in 2015, she was dismissed.

A change that has endured is the addition of women to the Shura Council. Until 2013, the Shura Council, a 150-member body that advises the king, was an all-male body. In 2013, King Abdullah declared that women would make up 20 percent of the Council and proceeded to appoint thirty women. The women must enter and exit the council building through separate doors and sit in a section reserved only for women, but it is a breakthrough nonetheless.

With respect to women and elections, there are not many opportunities because there are no national or provincial elections, only municipal elections for councils that do not have legislative power. Nonetheless, thanks to women's organizing and a subsequent decree issued by the late King Abdullah, in 2015—for the first time in the nation's history—women were granted the right to register to vote and to run for seats on these municipal councils.

But in the elections, women candidates were at a disadvantage when it came to campaigning. They could not directly address male voters but had to speak to them from behind screens to comply with strict segregation laws. And 90 percent of the voting pool were men. Twenty-one women were elected, which is barely 1 percent of the 2,106 municipal council seats that were up for grabs, and an additional seventeen women were appointed.

When the councils started to meet, the women were ordered to sit in separate rooms from the men and participate by video link. Two women in Jeddah who insisted on being at the same table with men received death threats and were forced to back down.[25]

Still, the elections were hailed as a victory by the Saudi and international press.

Some women thought the municipal elections were window dressing and boycotted them. "How could I be elected if I can't drive, if I can't have the right to custody of my children, if women are half citizens in this country?" asked university lecturer Aziza al-Yousef. "I think we need to change the whole system."[26]

Others disagree. "We shouldn't abandon practicing and engaging in any of our rights just because others are not yet attained," said Saudi scholar Hala Aldoeseri. "We have been working, studying and traveling without the rights to drive all our lives, that doesn't mean we should boycott other rights. Having women's voices in the municipalities is a step that can lead to more power sharing and more rights in the future."[27]

History professor and women's rights activist Hatoon al-Fassi, who has lobbied for ten years for women to have the right to vote, said it was a great psychological boost for Saudi women, particularly the candidates. "This is hugely significant. We have over 1,000 women convinced they can make a difference and who convinced their families to be part of this experience."[28]

Reem Asaad, a financial advisor from Jeddah, sent this tweet that went viral: "Voted! For the 1st time in my adult public life in #SaudiArabia. You may find this laughable but hey, it's a start. #saudiwomenvote."

SO WHAT ARE THE PROSPECTS FOR CHANGE?

In Saudi society, the position of women is determined by a mix of religion, patriarchy, family honor, and state power, but these forces are not static. In fact, the intense segregation in Saudi society is actually something quite new.

The idea that by nature men are lustful and women seductive, so that being a good Muslim requires constant separation, is one that became prevalent when the government gave into the conservative clerics during the turbulent years of the 1980s.

There are elderly Saudi women who reminisce about the days before the 1980s when there was more mixing of the sexes and women could choose whether to be covered in public.[29] Today, the puritanical taboos are beginning to fray, especially for the wealthy. You can find places like five-star hotel and fancy restaurants that don't impose sex segregation.

So there is certainly reason to hope that Saudi society can evolve in a more liberal fashion. As more Saudi women enter the workforce, as more and more workplaces begin to bend the segregation rules, as more young women study abroad and return home unhappy with the endless restrictions on their freedom, there will be more pressure. In the meantime, for many Saudi women, the pace of change is excruciatingly slow.

CHAPTER 5: THE TRAGIC CONDITION OF MIGRANT WORKERS

You can't understand Saudi Arabia without understanding that it is a nation built and run by millions of foreign workers. In 2015, they made up one-third of the population and filled over half the jobs; in the private sector, foreign workers accounted for nearly 80 percent of employees. Meanwhile, the official unemployment rate for Saudis was 12 percent.[1]

Some foreigners, mostly men, have skilled jobs that are well compensated, such as Westerners in the oil industry. Others, particularly Asians, have low-skilled jobs in areas such as retail, construction, the service industry, or transportation. Many appreciate their jobs and have made Saudi Arabia their home. In fact, they may be the second or third generation of their families to live in Saudi Arabia.

Millions of others are migrants, mostly from poor families in Asia and Africa, who work for several years, send money back to their families, and then return home. They perform the menial, lowest-paid jobs that Saudis won't do for such low pay. It is here, in the underbelly of the labor system, that the worst conditions exist. Among the most vulnerable are unskilled male laborers and female domestic workers.

These workers are subjected to an abusive sponsorship system called *kafala* in which foreigners are bought, sold, and traded. The saga of human bondage in this oil-rich nation is tragic.

HOW DID THIS SYSTEM EVOLVE?

In the late 1930s, when oil was first discovered, the country needed both foreign expertise and labor to build up its immense oil reserves. In the years following World War II, foreign technical, professional, and administrative personnel, mainly from other Middle Eastern countries, were encouraged to work in the kingdom.

Even greater numbers of foreign workers arrived in the 1970s, when the nation's coffers were awash in petrodollars. The boom in infrastructure and development brought a flood of skilled and unskilled workers, and the rising incomes of Saudis led to an influx of foreign women to serve as domestic workers.

The first wave of migrants came primarily from Arab countries such as Palestine, Egypt, and Yemen, but also from Pakistan and India. In the early 1980s, Thailand, the Philippines, Sri Lanka, and Indonesia also furnished migrant workers. This flood of foreigners was so massive that it led to the doubling of the Saudi population between 1973 and 1985.[2]

HOW DOES THE MIGRANT SYSTEM WORK?

Slavery was not banned in Saudi Arabia until 1962, when there were still some thirty thousand slaves in the country. According to

Saudi scholar Ali al-Ahmed, a culture of slavery still pervades the country in the form of kafala, a system that ties the residency status of migrant workers to their employers, granting the latter total control. Human rights groups call this a form of indentured servitude.[3]

Many workers are lured to the kingdom under false pretenses, with promises of good pay and work conditions. Coming from poor countries, they often pay large fees to recruitment agencies in their home country and may be obligated to work several months just to pay off the fee.

Paying a recruitment fee, however, is not enough to secure entry into Saudi Arabia. Prospective workers must first obtain an *iqama*, a residency permit that allows them to work. This must be issued through a legal resident or Saudi national, who then becomes the *kafeel*, or sponsor. The sponsorship system is the legal foundation that binds a migrant worker to one individual. This sponsor has the power to alter the terms of the employment contract, transfer the contract to another employer without the worker's consent, repatriate the worker without prior notice, and ban the worker from reentering the country. Despite laws to the contrary, some employers still confiscate migrants' passports, withhold wages, and force them to work against their will.

Workers in this system who leave their employers are considered runaways, and can be arrested and deported. They are not even allowed to leave the country without an exit permit from the employer.[4]

Among these workers, there is a hierarchy of prejudice, with Africans on the bottom rung. Asians from the Philippines,

Malaysia, and Sri Lanka occupy a higher status, although all are mainly employed as unskilled laborers or domestic workers.

Abuses include excessive work hours, wages withheld for months or years on end, forced confinement, food deprivation, and psychological and physical abuse.

The workers' situations can become even more precarious if they fall outside the kafala system and live in the country illegally. Some migrant workers illegally leave their original employment to secure better terms with another employer or to escape from an abusive employer. Others simply get stuck in Saudi Arabia, unable to leave due to strict exit visa requirements, and therefore must work illegally to sustain themselves and their families back home.

Ra'id, a twenty-four-year-old Yemeni, entered Saudi Arabia legally after obtaining a visa to work for a cargo company. Unable to locate his sponsor after arriving, he worked, without a permit, at a gas station. When he finally located his sponsor, the sponsor denied the existence of the cargo company and demanded that he pay $1,000 for a residency card and work permit. Ra'id paid the money, but the Saudi sponsor never provided him with either a residency card or work permit, and threatened to report him to authorities if he made a fuss. Ra'id eventually decided to leave Saudi Arabia, but then had to pay the sponsor another $1,000 to obtain an exit visa.

Amin, thirty-four, a migrant worker from Yemen, went to Saudi Arabia in 2011 to work in construction. He paid $640 to obtain the visa, but when he arrived in Saudi Arabia his sponsor demanded an additional $2,667 to obtain his residency card and work permit. When he refused to pay, his sponsor took him to the government's immigration center to be deported

Undocumented workers have nowhere to go to seek redress. The employer of Mahmoud, a twenty-seven-year-old Yemeni who entered Saudi Arabia illegally in 2011, gave him no medical assistance when he lost his right arm in an accident while operating heavy machinery at a rock quarry. "My arm was cut off while I was working at the controls of a heavy machine," Mahmoud recalled. "An Indian worker drove me to the hospital. I heard the Saudi boss tell the Indian over the phone to tell the police I was in a car accident, which he did. I told the police the truth, but they did not believe me. I had two operations to stop the bleeding, and after that I was chained to the hospital bed for two-and-a-half months." When he was strong enough to get up, Mahmoud was deported.[5]

WHAT IS THE SITUATION FOR FEMALE DOMESTIC WORKERS?

In 2013, the International Labor Organization estimated that Saudi Arabia was one of the largest employers of domestic workers in the world.[6] Most are hired by individual families to clean, cook, do laundry, and care for children and the elderly.

Wealthy Saudis were the first to import domestic workers, but with the 1973 oil boom, domestic workers also became common in the homes of the newly emerging middle class. It became a matter of prestige to have several workers, especially from English-speaking countries such as the Philippines. Some families preferred Muslim women, many of whom came from Indonesia or Bangladesh.

The average monthly salary for a domestic worker varies according to nationality, race, religion, and experience, and in 2015 it ranged between about $200 to $400 dollars. A typical workday is fifteen hours, which works out to less than a dollar an hour.[7]

Most Saudi women still don't work outside the home, yet they hire foreigners to do household chores. This is often true even in middle-class families. "It is important for Saudi women to feel that they are not at the bottom of the social hierarchy, as there is always another woman who is much worse off than themselves," says author Madawi al-Rasheed. "In popular imagination, Saudi women are 'jewels,' protected and cared for as they increasingly become managers of the household with its many servants rather than cooks and cleaners."[8]

While domestic workers suffer abuses worldwide, tales abound about the particularly horrific abuses they suffer at the hands of Saudi employers, both inside the kingdom and abroad.

In 2010, doctors in Sri Lanka operated on forty-nine-year-old Lahadapurage Daneris Ariyawathie to remove twenty-four nails her Saudi employers had hammered into her hands, legs, and forehead after she complained to them about being overworked.[9]

Also in 2010, an Indonesian maid said her Saudi employer cut and burned her face with scissors and a hot iron, leaving her with disfiguring, lifelong injuries.[10]

In 2014, photos went viral of a Filipina domestic worker's horrific injuries from boiling water that her employer's mother threw on her for not making coffee fast enough.[11]

In 2015, Kasturi Munirathinam, a domestic worker from Tamil Nadu, India, tried to flee her work after she was consistently denied pay and barely given enough to eat. After her employer locked her inside, she tried to escape by climbing out a window using her sari as a rope. Her employer hacked off her hand, and she fell from the third floor, injuring her spine. Video of Munirathinam lying in her Saudi hospital bed was shown on television in India and sparked an outcry, forcing the Indian government to bring her home.[12]

A domestic worker from Kenya had to choose between having sex with her boss or being killed by him. "I felt like a prostitute," she recalled. "I used to obey because I wanted to come back to my country safely."[13]

These are cases where the worker survived. In other instances, domestic workers have died while trying to escape abusive conditions, committed suicide, been beaten to death by their employers, or beheaded by the state.

In 2011, a fifty-four-year-old Indonesian worker, Ruyati Binti Satubi Saruna, was accused of killing her employer. She was tried, sentenced, and decapitated by sword without being able to consult her government.[14] Forty-five Indonesian maids were said to be on death row in 2013.[15]

WHAT HAPPENS WHEN FOREIGN WORKERS REPORT ABUSES?

When workers report abuses, the employers rarely face criminal charges and courts seldom convict them. Migrants, most of whom do not speak Arabic, may be denied access to translators and lawyers, and often are not allowed to contact their embassies. In cases that Human Rights Watch has documented, Saudi authorities failed to provide migrants consistent access to interpreters and lawyers at police stations and during legal proceedings. Authorities prohibit domestic workers from working until the conclusion of their criminal cases, which may take years.

Domestic workers may also have to deal with fake or fabricated counteraccusations by former employers, including theft or "sorcery," which often forces workers to drop their own charges. With no shelters for abused domestic workers, those who escape abuse end up in overcrowded embassy shelters or deportation centers. Many drop their criminal complaints and return home without any savings, and without any justice.[16]

WHY HAVE THERE BEEN CAMPAIGNS TO DEPORT MIGRANT WORKERS?

The Saudi government has tried to reduce the nation's reliance on foreign workers, especially with the high rate of unemployment among Saudi nationals. Saudis, however, do not want to take the difficult, low-paying jobs that foreigners are willing to perform.

As for skilled jobs, the Saudi system of education, which emphasizes religion and rote learning, has not prepared its students well for the modern economy.

The government has attempted various solutions to increase employment for Saudis, from reducing the flow of foreign workers to improving the educational system to creating incentives for Saudi businesses to hire locals. In 2000, as part of a policy of "Saudization," the government implemented the *Nitaqat* program, which says that businesses with more than twenty employees must employ at least 25 percent Saudis. The private sector largely ignored this decree because they have to pay Saudis more than double the salary of foreigners.

In 2013, the process of Saudization was accompanied by a sweeping campaign to detain and expel thousands of foreign workers without valid residency or work permits, or workers caught working for an employer other than their legal sponsor.

The campaign was brutal. Police raided neighborhoods and businesses, and set up checkpoints to check IDs. They beat and violently rounded up workers. Sadiyo, a Somali woman who was nine months pregnant, was detained and deported separately from her husband. She told Human Rights Watch that a Saudi policewoman beat her on the back with a baton while she stood in line at Jeddah airport, sending her into labor. She gave birth on the floor of the plane as it flew to Mogadishu.[17] There were reports of migrant women being gang raped by vigilantes and Saudi police.

Saudi authorities arbitrarily confiscated workers' personal property, forcing many migrants to return to their home countries destitute, without even money for food or transportation to their villages.

The detention and deportation campaign was accompanied by a racist backlash against migrants, especially in urban areas with large foreign populations. In November 2015, an attack on migrants by Saudi citizens armed with sticks, swords, machetes, and firearms resulted in the death of at least three Ethiopians.

WHAT CAN BE DONE TO TRY TO STOP THESE ABUSES?

Embarrassed by international criticism, the Saudi government has tried to improve work conditions. In 2013, new regulations for domestic workers granted them the right to nine hours of rest every day, one day off a week, and one month of paid vacation every two years. The regulations are difficult to enforce because the workers live in people's homes, hidden from view. Also, these rules still allow domestic workers to work up to fifteen hours a day, they still require workers to have permission from their employers to simply leave the country, and migrant workers who change jobs without their employer's approval still risk becoming illegal, and therefore subject to deportation.

In 2014, the government established a new online portal that gives domestic workers access to information regarding their legal rights, and a "helpline" for resources to access labor dispute courts. The Ministry of Labor produced a multilingual guidebook that is supposed to be distributed to all migrant workers entering the

MEDEA BENJAMIN

country, with a telephone number for workers to report abuses. Additionally, Saudi police are supposed to have an anti-trafficking hotline with operators who speak Arabic and English.

The following year, 2015, more labor laws were passed, including provisions increasing paid leave and compensation for job-related injuries, and giving the Labor Ministry greater inspection and enforcement powers. They increased penalties for abusive employers, including fines for withholding employees' passports, not paying salaries on time, violating health and safety standards, and employing children under fifteen. *Arab News* reported that in 2015, the Labor Ministry had shut down 1,441 companies for violating the labor laws.[18] But there is one huge flaw with the 2015 labor laws —they exclude both domestic workers and short-term migrant workers who enter the country for two months or less.

Some of the most effective campaigns to help migrant workers have come from grassroots activists inside Saudi Arabia and abroad. They circulate videos and photos of abuses. A video of an employer at a brick-making factory beating three young Indian men with a plank was seen by over a million viewers.[19] Another video of a Saudi man groping and sexually harassing his maid, filmed and posted by the man's wife as a way to shame him, went viral.[20] There are numerous online petitions and Twitter campaigns, such as #SomeoneTellSaudiArabia, started by an Ethiopian to demand that Saudis stop beating and beheading migrant workers. Returning home, some workers have told their gruesome stories to local news media, causing an uproar. Migrant worker organizations have sprung up to encourage people not to seek employment in Saudi Arabia and to push their governments to do more to protect their citizens abroad.

Since there is so much money coming back home from workers' remittances, governments are often reluctant to stand up to the Saudis. But sometimes the outcry is so widespread that they are forced to act. In 2015, when the Saudi government beheaded two Indonesian domestic workers accused of murder, the outpouring of anger propelled the Indonesian government to announce a ban on sending domestic workers to Saudi Arabia and other Gulf states. Similar bans have been imposed in Kenya, Ethiopia, and Uganda. In 2015, the Indian government, pressured by women's groups disgusted by the treatment—including rape—of Indian migrant workers, was also considering a ban.

Unfortunately, desperate workers and devious recruitment agencies will always find ways to circumvent these bans. The real solutions must come from inside Saudi Arabia. The Saudi government needs to abolish the kafala sponsorship system so that workers are not tied to their sponsors. It needs to abolish the "exit visa" requirement that makes it hard for workers to leave the country. It needs to ensure that domestic workers have equal labor law protections, and it needs to investigate and prosecute abusive employers and recruiters. Fledgling Saudi activist groups need to be supported so that they become more effective advocates. Only then will there be any hope of seeing an end to this twenty-first-century version of slavery.

CHAPTER 6: SPREADING WAHHABISM, SUPPORTING EXTREMISM

Certainly Saudi Arabia is not the only culprit for the worldwide surge in violent Muslim extremism since 2000. There are the catastrophic U.S. wars in Iraq, Afghanistan, and Libya; the illegal Israeli occupation of the Palestinian territories; the sectarian nature of the Iraqi government; the torture at Guantanamo Bay and Abu Ghraib; and the brutal repression of the Assad dictatorship in Syria. But Wahhabi ideology has certainly been one of the key factors in the spread of extremism.

WHAT IS WAHHABISM AND WHAT ARE ITS ORIGINS?

Wahhabism is an extreme, fundamentalist sect of Sunni Islam that was created based on the teachings of eighteenth-century Imam Wahhab. His students and followers advocated a return to the austere practices supposedly followed by the Salaf, or earliest Muslims, during the seventh century.

According to Imam Wahhab, popular local forms of Islam that incorporated reverence to past Imams, their shrines, or ancient pagan sacred sites were sacrilegious, since only the one true God is worthy of reverence. The Shia practice of revering and making pilgrimages to the shrines of Shiite Imams was one of Wahhab's prime targets, but he also condemned Sunni Muslims in Arabia for revering trees, rocks, and other traditional sacred sites. Based on his teachings, Wahhabism developed in its harshest form to say that Muslims should hate non-Muslims; that Shia and other non-Wahhabi Muslims are infidels; and that the Saudi monarchy is the ordained protector of the Muslim faith.[1]

The interpretation of Islam promoted by the Saudis was in sharp contrast to the ancient traditions of tolerance in Muslim countries like Indonesia, Malaysia, and Mali. President Obama himself remarked on this in a conversation with Australian Prime Minister Malcolm Turnbull. Obama described how he has watched Indonesia, where he lived as a child, gradually move from a "relaxed, syncretistic Islam to a more fundamentalist, unforgiving interpretation" due to Saudi influence.[2]

The name "Wahhabism" itself was originally used only by Imam Wahhab's opponents, much as opponents of today's Islamic State movement call it by the acronym "Daesh." Calling Wahhab's followers "Wahhabis" was a sly dig at the contradiction at the heart of this new sect. The Wahhabis condemned reverence to other well-known Imams, but seemed to make an exception for Wahhab himself, so the label "Wahhabi" was pointedly ironic.

Wahhabism would have remained a marginal sect were it not for its union with the political power of the Saudi family combined with oil money. Wahhabism was first used by the Al Saud

MEDEA BENJAMIN

family as a way to unite the peninsula's unruly tribes and later as a bulwark against the rise of secularism, Arab nationalism, and Soviet influence in the Middle East. Wahhabism became the strategy for the monarchy to justify its hold on power and project that power abroad.

As the kingdom evolved, the Saudi family and religious clerics used the public schools to inculcate their citizens with the radical Wahhabist ideology. According to a 2006 report by the U.S. group Freedom House, Islamic studies textbooks issued by the Saudi Ministry of Education taught students that Christians, Jews, Shiites, and Sufi Muslims are enemies of the true believer. An eighth grade text read: "The apes are Jews, the people of the Sabbath; while the swine are the Christians, the infidels of the communion of Jesus." Some books justified violence against apostates, sorcerers, and homosexuals, and labeled Jews and Christians "enemies of the believers." A high school textbook presented the "Protocols of the Elders of Zion" as an authentic document, rather than a notorious forgery designed to promote hostility toward Jews.[3]

Responding to U.S. pressure, the Saudis agreed to revise and update textbooks to remove bigoted views. They pledged to complete the task in two years, but eight years later, in 2014, the U.S. Commission on International Religious Freedom reported that "revisions are incomplete and language promoting hatred and incitement to violence remains in high school texts."[4] It is also impossible to recall the tens of thousands of older versions of textbooks and other intolerant materials in circulation.

Wahhabi-oriented television channels that reach deep into households from urban Tunisia to rural Mali continue to spew hate, as do some Islamist newspapers and websites. The tragic result is that in some parts of the world, a whole generation of Muslims has grown up with a distorted, negative view of other religions and an intolerant, sectarian understanding of their own faith.

Throughout world history, such unions of political power and religious sects have created powerful and dangerous forces. The claims of fundamentalists to represent "pure" forms of well-established religions have made these political movements particularly resistant to compromise or reconciliation with the rest of human society.

These patterns have emerged in the United States with the Religious Right, in Latin America with Evangelical Christians, in Sri Lanka with the Sinhalese Buddhist Nationalists, in India with the Hindu Nationalist BJP, in Israel with the fundamentalist Jewish sects colonizing illegal settlements, and in Iraq with the U.S.-backed Da'wa regime.

These movements share several common features:

They claim to be carrying out the will of God or a divine plan.

They condemn members of other branches of their own religion as heathens or apostates.

They justify war, murder, and other crimes as a legitimate means to religiously sanctioned political ends.

They harness religious authority to justify their own political and economic interests.

The rise of Saudi Arabia and the spread of Sunni fundamentalism may be the clearest example of this pattern in the world today, and it poses a grave threat to global security and peace

HOW DID WAHHABISM SPREAD BEYOND THE ARABIAN PENINSULA?

The year 1979 was critical in Saudi history. The Iranian revolution, the seizure of the Grand Mosque in Mecca by Saudi militants, and the Soviet invasion of Afghanistan all became intertwined in determining the path Saudi rulers would take.

The Iranian revolution sent shock waves through the Saudi leadership, not only because the Iranian clerics staked a competitive claim to representing Islam, but also because it inspired Wahhabi militants inside the kingdom to question Saudi rulers. This led to the November 1979 seizure of the Grand Mosque in Mecca by religious extremists. Their call for the overthrow of the royal family, who they claimed had been corrupted by Western interests, echoed the revolutionaries who deposed the Shah in neighboring Iran.

Militants held the mosque for two weeks with hundreds of pilgrims trapped inside. The Saudi rulers eventually brought in French special forces to recapture the mosque. In the bloody battle that ensued, hundreds were killed—rebels, Saudi forces, and pilgrims—and the government later beheaded sixty-three captured militants in public squares across the country.[5]

Facing a crisis in the wake of the Iranian revolution and Grand Mosque seizure, the Saudi rulers calculated that one way to help reclaim their role as the rightful guardians of Islam in the region—and appease their own religious zealots—would be by using their oil wealth to spread Wahhabi ideology all over the world. They also used the Soviet invasion of Afghanistan to redirect the religious zeal of Saudi militants toward external conflicts, encouraging them to go fight against the Soviet infidels.

The soaring oil prices in the 1970s gave the kingdom all the petrodollars it needed to export its rigid form of Islam. The Muslim World League, established by the Saudis in 1962 to spread Islamic teachings, became a powerhouse for the production and dissemination of Wahhabi scholarship around the globe. The Saudi Ministry of Religion printed and distributed Wahhabi translations of the Quran and Wahhabi doctrinal texts throughout the Middle East, Africa, and Asia. Saudis gained control of most Islamic publishing houses around the world.

They built *madrassas*, which means schools in Arabic, to teach Wahhabi ideology throughout the Muslim world. In many poor regions, this was the only education available. One of the countries that received the largest number of Saudi schools was Pakistan. General Zia-ul-Haq had seized power in 1977, imposed Sharia law, and then gave the Saudis free rein to create Islamic schools across the country to fill the gap of a collapsed education system.

According to the late King Fahd's website, the Saudi government spent $4 billion a year building mosques and schools, paying the salaries of preachers and teachers, providing scholarships for students, and publishing textbooks to spread Wahhabism. Together with Wahhabi charities and royal trusts, they built more than fifteen hundred mosques, two hundred Muslim centers, two hundred Islamic colleges, and two thousand madrassas worldwide. The Saudi government staffed those institutions with nearly four thousand preachers and missionaries, paying for the salaries of students who received scholarships to study in the kingdom and returned home to teach in schools or preach in mosques.[6]

WHAT ROLE DID SAUDI ARABIA PLAY IN THE CREATION AND GROWTH OF THE TALIBAN?

When Afghanistan, another largely Sunni country, came under Soviet domination in 1979, the Saudi monarchy saw an opportunity to position itself as the global defender of Muslims against foreign invaders. This was also convenient for the United States, whose main concern was defeating the Soviet Union.

In collaboration with the CIA, the Saudis funded the armed resistance in Afghanistan, a group that became known as the *mujahideen*, which translates to "holy warriors." The United States committed hundreds of millions of dollars each year to the mission, and the Saudis matched it, dollar for dollar, with their money flowing through a CIA-run Swiss bank account.[7]

The Saudis also helped recruit fighters for the resistance by creating a new kind of madrassa in the Pakistan–Afghanistan region that focused more on making war on infidels (the Soviets) than on Islamic scholarship. The recruits came predominantly from the lower classes in the Afghan–Pakistan region, including Afghans who had fled the Soviet invasion and were living in refugee camps.

Thousands of these schools sprang up along Pakistan's border and then inside Afghanistan itself—training not scholars, but fighters equipped with Wahhabi ideology and American weapons. They used Islam as a vehicle for creating a very disciplined guerrilla army with a clear anti-communist ideology.

In these camps, a new generation came of age, calling themselves the Taliban, which comes from the Arabic word *talib*, which means student. They became one of the groups of mujahideen that fought the Soviet occupation from 1979 to 1989.

When the Soviets withdrew, Afghanistan plunged into chaos with competing warlords fighting each other for control. The Taliban, who had been loosely organized on a regional basis, unified under the leadership of Mullah Omar, the son of a landless farmer. From Pakistan, they launched an offensive and succeeded in seizing the city of Kandahar from a notorious warlord. Two years later, they took Kabul and declared the establishment of the Islamic Emirate of Afghanistan.

Only three countries—Pakistan, the United Arab Emirates, and Saudi Arabia—established diplomatic relations with the new Taliban government. The Saudi government even granted government-paid holidays to its employees and their families to visit Afghanistan so they could witness the "true Islam." In 1998, the Saudi monarch invited Mullah Omar to make the Hajj to Mecca.[8]

A well-known Saudi figure who supported the Taliban and set up operations in Afghanistan during that time was Osama bin Laden. After helping the mujahideen overthrow the Soviets, bin Laden had started thinking about a global jihad. At a 1988 meeting in Peshawar, Pakistan, he and some of his top fighters decided to form a new network and called it Al Qaeda—literally, "the Base." They forged links with militants across the Middle East and North Africa. After a stint in Sudan, bin Laden returned to Afghanistan in 1996 and was warmly welcomed by the Taliban and its top leader Mullah Omar.

It was from the Al Qaeda headquarters in Afghanistan that bin Laden announced a jihad to expel foreign troops and interests from Islamic lands, and made a public declaration of war against the United States.

WHAT WAS THE SAUDI INVOLVEMENT IN THE 9/11 ATTACKS?

To this day, there is no clarity about the role of the Saudi government or individual Saudis with close ties to the government in the 9/11 attacks. We know that fifteen of the nineteen hijackers were Saudi. We know that the bin Laden family had close ties to the family of George Bush. We know that right after the attack, wealthy Saudis living in the United States frantically contacted the Saudi Embassy in Washington asking to leave because they feared a backlash. Within days of the attack, some 140 Saudis, including about two dozen members of the bin Laden family, were spirited out of the country with little questioning by the FBI.[9] But there is much that remains unknown.

There have been claims that Saudi Arabia's ruling elite, under the guise of support for Islamic charities, distributed money to Sunni extremists inside the United States in the run-up to the September 11 attacks. One of the hijackers, Omar al-Bayoumi, was a student who seemed to have access to large amounts of money from Saudi Arabia. An FBI source identified al-Bayoumi as the person who delivered $400,000 from Saudi Arabia to a mosque in San Diego.[10]

The allegations were bolstered when former Al Qaeda operative Zacarias Moussaoui accused prominent members of Saudi Arabia's royal family of being major donors to the terrorist network in the late 1990s—allegations that Saudi officials denied.

Answers to some of these questions might be found in the 2002 Congressional Joint Inquiry into the terrorist attacks. The 838-page investigation was completed in December 2002, but the Bush administration refused to release it until after its invasion of Iraq, and refused to declassify a twenty-eight-page portion of the report that supposedly dealt with Saudi Arabia and the financing of the attacks. For years, President Obama promised 9/11 family members that he would help them get the section released, but never did. In May 2016, with renewed attention on the issue, he promised a decision in a month.

Members of Congress are allowed to read the twenty-eight pages in a secure, soundproof facility in the basement of the Capitol, but they are not allowed to take notes, bring any staff, or talk about the content. After reading the twenty-eight pages, Representative Thomas Massie from Kentucky said, "They're the most consequential pages in the thousand-page report." Massie said that the section was "shocking" and that he had to "stop every couple pages and try to rearrange my understanding of history."[11]

Former Senator Bob Graham, who chaired the investigation, said, "The twenty-eight pages primarily relate to who financed 9/11, and they point a very strong finger at Saudi Arabia as being the principal financier."[12] Graham has been advocating for the pages to be made public and suggested that the Bush and Obama administrations have refused to release the information for fear of alienating an influential military and economic partner.

Senator Graham's focus on the Saudi connection received renewed attention in 2015 with a federal court case in which 9/11 family members claimed Saudi Arabia was responsible for aiding the hijackers.

In sworn statements for the lawsuit, Graham said there was evidence that the Saudi government supported the terrorists. He also said the FBI withheld from his commission's inquiry the fact that the bureau had investigated a Saudi family in Sarasota, Florida, and had found multiple contacts between the Saudi family and the hijackers training nearby, and that the family fled the country just before the attacks. "One thing that irritates me is that the FBI has gone beyond just covering up into what I call aggressive deception," Graham said.[13]

Many people dispute Graham's interpretation and insist the Saudi government had no ties to the attacks. They point to a separate Congressional study in 2004 by the 9/11 Commission that found no evidence that the Saudi government or senior Saudi officials individually funded Al Qaeda.[14]

In May 2016, however, John Lehman, a Republican who served as U.S. Navy Secretary in the Reagan administration and was among the ten commission members, said there was, indeed, clear evidence that Saudi government employees helped some of the 9/11 hijackers. He said the commission investigated at least five Saudi government officials, including employees of the kingdom's Ministry of Islamic Affairs, who potentially aided some of the hijackers.

There have been numerous attempts by members of Congress to urge President Bush and later President Obama to declassify the twenty-eight pages, arguing that the American people have the right to know the extent of Saudi involvement in the attacks. A 2015 bill in the House, H.Res.14, which urged Obama to release the pages, was introduced with bipartisan support and garnered forty-one cosponsors, but never made it to the floor for a vote. It was reintroduced in 2016.

Also introduced was a bill promoted by 9/11 widows who want to sue Saudi Arabia in U.S. courts but have been blocked by the Foreign Sovereign Immunities Act. The bill, called the Justice

Against Sponsors of Terrorism Act or JASTA, would strip immunity from countries potentially involved in acts of terrorism on U.S. soil. While the bill had broad bipartisan support, President Obama vowed to veto it out of concerns over international retribution. The Saudi government threatened that if the bill passed, they would withdraw $750 billion in Saudi investments in U.S. assets.

The Saudi threats unleashed a new wave of anger from 9/11 families, who denounced Saudi blackmail and President Obama's capitulation. "We struggle to understand why the U.S. government, led by President Obama, would so willingly drop to its knees and bare its neck to the shiny sword of Saudi extortion," said an angry Kristen Breitweiser, one of the "Jersey Girls" whose husband died on 9/11. "What has become of our country? America needs elected officials who recognize that U.S. citizens are their constituents—not oil-rich nations that bankroll terrorists."

No matter what happens with the twenty-eight pages and the 9/11 families' lawsuits, one thing is certain: The Wahhabist ideology that defines Saudi Arabia has spawned leaders like Osama bin Laden, and terrorist groups like Al Qaeda. The 9/11 attacks are a direct outgrowth of this fundamentalist ideology.

WHAT ARE THE SAUDI TIES WITH EXTREMIST SUNNI GROUPS WORLDWIDE?

Many young men who studied in Saudi madrassas overseas and got their training in the Afghan war carried their intolerant ideology and military training back to their native lands, starting branches of Al Qaeda or other extremist groups across the Middle East, northern Africa, and various parts of Asia.

In addition, always anxious to direct the anger of Saudi citizens outward, Saudi rulers continued to encourage their own young men to wage jihad overseas. In the 1980s, the plight of oppressed Muslims from Palestine and Lebanon to Bosnia and Chechnya was broadcast on state television and taught in mosques as a way of whipping up feverish support for fighting abroad. A survey of Saudi men who volunteered to fight in Afghanistan, Bosnia, or Chechnya, or to train in Al Qaeda camps, found that most were motivated by the desire to help their suffering Muslim brothers and sisters.[15]

Saudi officials, religious groups, charities, and private individuals became prolific sponsors of international terrorist groups as disparate as the Taliban, Al Qaeda, the Pakistani Lashkar-e-Tayyiba (LeT), and the Al-Nusra Front in Syria. In 2008, a U.S. Treasury official testified in a congressional hearing that Saudi Arabia was the location from which more money was going to Sunni terror groups than from any other place in the world.[16]

A WikiLeaks-revealed 2009 cable quotes then–Secretary of State Hillary Clinton as saying: "Donors in Saudi Arabia constitute the most significant source of funding to Sunni terrorist groups worldwide. . . . More needs to be done since Saudi Arabia remains a critical financial support base for Al Qaeda, the Taliban, Lashkar e-Tayyiba and other terrorist groups." Three other Arab countries listed as sources of militant money were Qatar, Kuwait, and the United Arab Emirates, all neighbors of Saudi Arabia and members of the Gulf Cooperation Council (GCC).[17]

The Pakistani Lashkar-e-Tayyiba, the group that carried out the 2008 attacks in Mumbai, India, that left 164 dead, used a Saudi-based front company to fund its activities. A study of suicide bombers working with Al Qaeda in Iraq from 2006 to 2007, during the U.S. occupation, found that the largest group of foreigner suicide bombers were Saudis, and that Saudi fighters contributed the greatest amount of money to Al Qaeda in Iraq.[18]

The Saudi version of Islam has also had a negative impact in Africa. Islam has had a strong presence in Africa, particularly Northern Africa, dating all the way back to 615 A.D. when the first Muslims immigrated to what is now Ethiopia to escape persecution. Sufism became a popular form of Islam, a form that promoted ethnic, linguistic, and cultural diversity, as well as peace and harmony. But in the tumultuous political climate of postcolonial Africa, Saudi Arabia began reaching its tentacles of extremism into the region.

The Saudi government spent billions of dollars funding mosques and religious schools from Somalia and Senegal to Mali and Nigeria, and awarding scholarships for students to study in the kingdom. Returning home, many students criticized the Sufi tradition and instead spread Wahhabi views. In Mali, the Saudi-based World Assembly of Muslim Youth built a massive Islamic education center in Bamako. The failed economies and high unemployment that has plagued Africa for decades has made many young men vulnerable to the rising presence of extremist groups like Al Qaeda.

The worst example of Saudi influence in Africa has been in Nigeria. In 2002, a charismatic cleric named Mohammed Yusuf created Boko Haram as an alternative to Western education, which he claimed undermined Nigeria's development. Boko Haram literally means "Western education is a sin."

About that time, Osama bin Laden sent an aide to Nigeria with $3 million to give to local groups that shared Al Qaeda's mission to impose Islamic rule. One of the main groups he funded was Boko Haram, and when the Nigerian government cracked down on the group, Yusuf took refuge in Saudi Arabia. Boko Haram turned into a fanatic, extremist group that has carried out vicious terrorist attacks against government officials and civilians, including the 2014 kidnapping of 276 schoolgirls. Boko Haram was affiliated with Al Qaeda until 2015, when the group switched its allegiance to the Islamic State.

The radicalization of Muslim youth in Europe, particularly Belgium, can also be traced back to the Saudis. The terrorists who attacked both Paris in 2015 and Belgium in 2016 came from the area of Belgium where Saudi influence is pronounced. In 1967 a deal was struck between King Baudouin of Belgium and Saudi Arabia's King Faisal. In exchange for favorable oil concessions, the Belgian government let the Saudis take over a large pavilion in Brussels and convert it into the Great Mosque and cultural center. For years Saudi-trained clerics used the space to spread

Wahhabism, which had an influence on the more moderate Muslim immigrants from Morocco and Turkey.

A WikiLeaks disclosure of classified Saudi documents found that in 2012, the Belgian government had asked Saudi authorities to remove Khalid Al Abri, who was director of Belgium's Great Mosque but also a Saudi Embassy employee, for propagating intolerant Sunni radicalism.[19]

The German Vice-Chancellor Sigmar Gabriel was blunt in his attack on Saudi-funded mosques in the West. "We have to make clear to the Saudis that the time of looking away is over," he said in 2015. "Wahhabi mosques all over the world are financed by Saudi Arabia. In Germany, many dangerous Islamists come from these communities."[20]

WHAT IS THE SAUDI CONNECTION TO THE ISLAMIC STATE?

After the 2011 popular uprising against Bashar al-Assad in Syria, Saudi clerics declared jihad against Assad, who is from a Shia-related sect called Alawites, and urged all Sunni Muslims to join the fight. Many Saudis heeded the call and joined extremist groups like al-Nusra (Al Qaeda's official Syrian affiliate), Ahrar ash-Sham (also linked to Al Qaeda), and the Islamic State, a group that represents Wahhabism taken to its extreme.

In 2014, the Saudi Interior Ministry estimated that at least twelve hundred Saudis had gone to Syria to join the Islamic State. Independent estimates suggested the figure was greater than twenty-five hundred.[21] According to a CIA report, between 2011 and 2015 nearly thirty thousand foreign fighters had joined the Islamic State from more than one hundred countries. The largest number of fighters came from Tunisia; Saudi Arabia was number two.[22]

Initially, significant sectors of Saudi society supported these extremist groups, applauding their Sunni piety and staunch opposition to Shiism. In July 2014, the Saudi-owned *Al-Hayat* newspaper released an opinion poll claiming that an astounding 92 percent of respondents believed that the Islamic State "conforms to the values of Islam and Islamic law."[23]

Donors from Saudi Arabia and other Gulf states channeled hundreds of millions of dollars to Syrian-based groups, including the Islamic State. In 2014, U.S. Vice President Joe Biden got in hot water when he said that the biggest problem in Syria was our allies. Speaking to students at Harvard's Kennedy School about the Saudis, Turks, and Emiratis, he said, "They were so determined to take down Assad and essentially have a proxy Sunni–Shia war, what did they do? They poured hundreds of millions of dollars and thousands of tons of weapons into anyone who would fight against Assad—except that the people who were being supplied were al-Nusra and Al Qaeda and the extremist elements of jihadis coming from other parts of the world. . . . We could not convince our colleagues to stop supplying them."[24] Biden was forced to apologize, but he spoke the truth: U.S. allies like the Saudis were indeed supporting the very extremists that the U.S. military was trying to defeat.

A 2014 study by the Washington Institute concluded that there was no credible evidence that the Saudi government itself was financially supporting the Islamic State, but found significant donations from private Saudi citizens, despite the government's efforts to block them. These funds played a particularly important role in the group's initial development.[25]

Lax banking regulations, traditional money-transfer networks, and influential sympathizers on the Arabian Peninsula allowed private funds to continue flowing, especially when funneled through third parties. According to the State Department, groups outside Saudi Arabia with ties to extremists made sophisticated use of social media to solicit donations from Saudi donors.

Tragically, in their eagerness to wage war by proxy against Assad and his Shia backers, the Saudis assisted the growth of the Islamic State, a monster that is now attacking their own regime.

HAVE TERRORIST GROUPS ATTACKED SAUDI ARABIA ITSELF?

Militant groups affiliated with Al Qaeda and the Islamic State are not only wreaking havoc outside the kingdom, but inside Saudi Arabia itself, threatening the nation's much-vaunted stability.

Scores of terrorist attacks occurred in the kingdom during the height of the Al Qaeda insurgency between 2000 and 2015. During this time, there were about sixty terrorist incidents within Saudi borders in which either Saudi citizens or foreign residents were killed or injured. They included the 2004 Al Qaeda attack on the U.S. Consulate in Jeddah that killed five U.S. government employees and wounded fourteen, the 2007 murders of three French nationals during a desert outing near the ancient city of Mada, and a 2014 attack on a remote Saudi–Yemeni border checkpoint, killing and wounding Saudi security officers.

Many of these militants were trained by Al Qaeda in the Arabian Peninsula (AQAP), a group based in Yemen and led by Saudi nationals. The State Department assessed in 2014 that AQAP had "continued its efforts to inspire sympathizers to support, finance, or engage in conflicts outside of Saudi Arabia and encouraged individual acts of terrorism within the Kingdom."[26]

The Saudis considered AQAP their number one threat until 2014, when AQAP was overshadowed by the Islamic State. Ironically, both groups were heavily influenced by the conservative Saudi ideology, but turned against the Saudi state for being pro-West, practicing rampant consumerism, being corrupt, and having deviated from the true beliefs of Wahhabism.

In 2015, Islamic State leader Abu Bakr al-Baghdadi announced his intention to expand the Islamic State to the "lands of al-Haramein," a reference to Mecca and Medina. He challenged Saudi leaders' credentials as defenders of Islam, calling them "the slaves of the Crusaders and allies of the Jews" and accusing them of abandoning Sunni Palestinians, Syrians, Iraqis, and others. He referred to the ruling family as "the serpent's head" and the "stronghold of the disease," likening them to the pre-Islamic pagan rulers of Mecca.[27]

MEDEA BENJAMIN

Baghdadi called on supporters inside the kingdom to target Saudi security forces, Shiites, and foreigners. In 2015 Islamic State supporters claimed responsibility for numerous deadly attacks, including the shooting of police officers, suicide bombing attacks on Shia mosques in the Eastern Province, a suicide bombing at a prison checkpoint, and an attack on Saudi security personnel in a mosque in the southwestern city of Abha.

WHAT IS THE SAUDI GOVERNMENT DOING TO STOP EXTREMIST GROUPS?

In 2014, the kingdom made it illegal for its citizens to support terrorist organizations, and took increased measures to prevent Saudis from travelling abroad to join extremist groups. It issued a decree setting prison sentences for anyone who fought on behalf of extremist groups, as well as individuals plotting attacks, recruiting, or fundraising for them. By the end of 2015, Saudi officials had arrested more than 1,600 suspected Islamic State supporters and claimed to have foiled several planned attacks.

The government gave $100 million to the United Nations Counter-Terrorism Center, an agency that was first proposed by King Abdullah in 2005 and formally inaugurated in 2011. It invested domestically in institutions designed to re-educate extremists, such as the Mohammed bin Nayef Center for Counseling and Care, the kingdom's showcase terrorist rehabilitation center that is named after the crown prince and Minister of the Interior.

Saudi officials claim these centers have a stellar record of rehabilitation through an intense program of education and job training. Opponents say these centers are like vacation resorts, with cushy living quarters where inmates are provided with swimming pools, art classes, conjugal visits, and financial support for their families. This royal treatment, they allege, reflects the government's sympathy for these jihadis, while jailed human rights activists are thrown into overcrowded, squalid cells with hardened criminals. They also insist that the program is not as successful as the government claims, since many inmates return to wage jihad. In 2014, Saudi police arrested eighty-eight suspected Al Qaeda operatives; fifty-nine of them had already been in the rehab program. Several months later, forty-seven of the seventy-seven individuals detained for their alleged connection to an Islamic State attack on a Shiite mosque were found to be former inmates of the center as well.[28]

The government also announced a crackdown on preachers who overtly supported the Islamic State. Saudi clerics had lagged far behind other Muslim scholars in denouncing terrorist groups. It was not until August 2014 that the Saudi Grand Mufti Sheikh Abdul-Aziz ibn Abdullah Al ash-Sheikh condemned the Islamic State and Al Qaeda, calling them the "first enemies of Muslims." He insisted that "the ideas of extremism, radicalism and terrorism do not belong to Islam in any way" and gave his approval to all efforts to combat Al Qaeda and the Islamic State.[29]

But many Saudi clerics still pray for the victory of the jihadis in Syria and Iraq; still ask God for help in defeating Shia, Christians, and Jews; and still preach views that feed sectarianism and anti-Western hatred.

Herein lies the rub: Even if Saudi Arabia was able to turn off the spigot of funds and resources, its Wahhabist foundation continues to form the basis of the extremist ideology the Islamic State preaches. Abd-al Wahhab's writings and commentaries on his works are distributed in the areas under the Islamic State's control. As Syrian and Iraqi towns fell to the Islamic State, Saudi textbooks replaced the books previously used in the classrooms.

In 2013, the European Union declared that Wahhabism was the main source of global terrorism. Former CIA director James Woolsey described Wahhabism as "the soil in which Al Qaeda and its sister terrorist organizations are flourishing."[30]

The Islamic State and Saudi Arabia are not enemies because they are ideologically incompatible, but rather because they threaten each other's interests. Islamic State leaders claim to have established a caliphate to which all pious Sunni Muslims owe allegiance, directly challenging the legitimacy of Saudi leaders who have long described themselves as the custodians of Islam's holiest sites and rulers of a state uniquely built on and devoted to the propagation of Sunni Islam.

In a powerful *New York Times* article in 2015, writer Kamel Daoud noted that in its struggle against terrorism, the West wages war on the Islamic State, but shakes hands with Saudi Arabia. "This is a mechanism of denial, and denial has a price: preserving the famous strategic alliance with Saudi Arabia at the risk of forgetting that the kingdom also relies on an alliance with a religious clergy that produces, legitimizes, spreads, preaches and defends Wahhabism, the ultra-puritanical form of Islam that Daesh [the Islamic State] feeds on."

He says the "mother" of the Islamic State is the invasion of Iraq; the "father" is Saudi Arabia and its religious-industrial complex. "Until that point is understood," Daoud insists, "battles may be won, but the war will be lost. Jihadists will be killed, only to be reborn again in future generations and raised on the same books."[31]

If world leaders really want to end the radicalization of Muslim youth and stop the spread of Wahhabi extremism, they must seriously address Saudi Arabia's religious-industrial complex.

CHAPTER 7: THE HISTORY OF SAUDI RELATIONS WITH THE UNITED STATES AND THE WEST

Despite the apparent mismatch between a liberal Western democracy and the fundamentalist Saudi monarchy, for decades U.S. presidents, both Democrat and Republican, have heralded their friendship with the royal Saudi family and vice versa. George W. Bush, with deep personal and financial ties to the royal family, was photographed kissing and holding hands with King Abdullah after the 9/11 attacks, despite having proclaimed: "We will make no distinction between the terrorists who committed these acts and those who harbored them."[1]

Relations under President Obama were less cozy for a variety of reasons: Saudi displeasure with the Iran nuclear deal, Saudi anger that Obama did not get more involved in overthrowing Syrian ruler al-Assad, Obama's comment in a magazine interview that Saudi Arabia and other U.S. allies in the Persian Gulf were "free riders," i.e., they didn't pay their fair share of military costs in the region.[2]

But these were merely wrinkles in the relationship, not cause for a breakup. After King Abdullah's death in January 2015, President Obama rushed to the king's funeral instead of joining forty heads of state at the Paris anti-terror solidarity march in the wake of the Charlie Hebdo attack. At the funeral, Obama spoke about the "genuine and warm friendship" between the two nations and called the relationship "a force for stability and security in the Middle East and beyond."[3]

WHAT ARE THE ORIGINS OF THE U.S.–SAUDI ALLIANCE?

From the very beginnings, the U.S.–Saudi relationship revolved around oil. A year after the creation of the Saudi state in 1932, U.S. companies had already gained permission from the king to drill for oil. The largest U.S. oil companies jumped into the action once major reserves were discovered, and brought the clout of the U.S. government along with them. The huge scale of the kingdom's energy output gave it enormous influence over energy markets, and the job of protecting Saudi Arabian oil became a cornerstone of U.S. foreign policy.

This became evident during World War II, when the United States began to see Saudi oil as critical for the running of the U.S. economy. Saudi Arabia was officially neutral during the war, but the U.S. government agreed to protect Saudi oil installations and King Saud approved a U.S. request to construct airfields in the kingdom.

The relationship between the governments was famously cemented in a 1945 meeting on the Suez Canal between President Franklin D. Roosevelt and King Abdulaziz, a meeting that shaped the destiny of the Middle East for decades to come. The two leaders agreed that the kingdom would supply the United States with oil, and the U.S. government would provide the kingdom with security and military assistance

After World War II, the two countries were allies in their opposition to Soviet "godless communism," with the United States focused on communism while the Saudis were more concerned about the "godless" side of the equation. They also collaborated to stop the spread of secular Arab nationalism that began sweeping the region in the 1950s. The U.S. choice to ally with the Saudi Islamists over secular nationalists, such as Egypt's Gamal Abdel Nasser and Iran's Mohammad Mosaddegh, is a decision that has cast a dark shadow on the region ever since.

Another shared interest between the United States and Saudi Arabia has been ensuring stable oil prices and the stability of the economies of Western countries, where Saudis had invested large sums of their oil revenue.

In 1973, a deal was struck between the two nations that every barrel of Saudi oil purchased, by any country, would be denominated in U.S. dollars. This meant that any country purchasing Saudi oil first had to exchange their own currency for U.S. dollars. By 1975, all the OPEC nations had agreed to follow suit. This helped shore up the U.S. economy by creating a tremendous demand for U.S. dollars. In addition, Saudi's excess oil profits were invested in the U.S. Treasury and U.S. banks and U.S. banks, a system known as "petrodollar recycling."

Over the years, U.S. presidents reiterated their commitments to Saudi Arabia's security. The 1947 Truman Doctrine, which stated that the United States would send military aid to countries threatened by Soviet communism, was used to strengthen U.S.–Saudi military ties. In 1950, President Truman told King Ibn Saud that the U.S. government was committed to preserving the territorial integrity of the monarchy. "No threat to your Kingdom could occur which would not be a matter of immediate concern to the United States," he promised.[4] This sentiment was reiterated in the 1957 Eisenhower Doctrine as well.

The 1969 Nixon Doctrine included aid to the three strategic U.S. allies in the region—Iran, Saudi Arabia, and Israel. Ten years later, after the U.S.-allied government in Iran was overthrown and the Soviets invaded Afghanistan, President Carter issued his Doctrine as a direct threat to the Soviets, essentially saying that the oil under the sands of the Middle East belonged to the United States and any nation that interfered would do so at their peril.

Carter's successor, Ronald Reagan, extended the policy in October 1981 with what is sometimes called the "Reagan Corollary to the Carter Doctrine," which proclaimed that the U.S. government would intervene to protect the Saudi rulers. While the Carter Doctrine focused on threats from forces outside the region, the Reagan Corollary pledged to secure the kingdom's internal stability.

So one by one, U.S. presidents promised to keep the Saudi Islamist theocracy in power. Were it not for this support, the Saudi monarchs might well have been overthrown long ago.

MEDEA BENJAMIN

HOW DID THE PRESENCE OF U.S. TROOPS ON SAUDI SOIL CONTRIBUTE TO THE 9/11 ATTACKS?

During the Soviet invasion of Afghanistan from 1979 to 1989, Saudi Arabia and the United States worked together to provide money, arms, and recruits to fight the Soviets. A major player in that effort was Saudi-born Osama bin Laden, the son of a prominent family with large interests in the construction industry and a privileged relationship to the House of Saud. Bin Laden joined with Saudi clerics to recruit Islamic militants from all over the Middle East to join the fight, supported by robust Saudi and U.S. funding. This group of guerilla fighters, the mujahideen, became the forefathers of Al Qaeda.

After the Soviets were defeated, bin Laden and other Saudi fighters returned home in 1990 to a hero's welcome. This was just before another war was about to break out, the 1991 Gulf War, when Iraq's Saddam Hussein invaded neighboring Kuwait. President George H. W. Bush declared war against Iraq for invading an ally nation (and putting U.S. oil interests at risk). The Saudi rulers, believing that Saddam Hussein might move his troops south in an attempt to control Saudi oil reserves, also declared war.

Osama bin Laden, with the network of fighters he had developed in the Afghan struggle, stepped up to offer his services to the Saudi rulers and convince them not to rely on the U.S. military to protect the nation. "I am ready to prepare one hundred thousand fighters with good combat capability within three months," he told the Saudi rulers. "You don't need Americans. You don't need any other non-Muslim troops. We will be enough."[5]

The U.S.–Saudi military alliance had long been a source of anguish for Saudi Islamists who viewed non-Muslims as infidels. The reaction of the Saudi monarchs fueled that anger. Not only did they turn down Osama bin Laden's offer, but they allowed more than five hundred thousand U.S. troops to flood into the Saudi desert. U.S. troops used Saudi soil as the launching pad for driving Saddam Hussein's Iraqi forces from Kuwait and the U.S. Air Force used Saudi bases to conduct an air campaign against Iraq. As part of the arrangement, the Saudi government also paid a major chunk of the costs of the war: around $36 billion of the $60 billion total.

Six weeks after the Gulf War started, the Iraqi troops were routed and retreated from Kuwait. President George H. W. Bush assured Saudi King Fahd that U.S. troops would withdraw from the kingdom once the war was over, but broke his promise. Instead, about five thousand U.S. combat troops and air crews stayed in Saudi military bases to enforce a "no-fly zone" in southern Iraq in an effort to support Iraq's Shia community against Saddam Hussein.

The presence of U.S. soldiers was an affront to many conservative Saudis. Osama bin Laden described it as a turning point in his life. He accused the Americans of defiling Saudi Holy Lands by violating the ban on drinking, the mixing of sexes, pornography, degenerate music, and crass consumerism. He denounced the Saudi rulers who allowed the continued U.S. military presence, which he considered a threat to Islam.

In 1994 bin Laden was stripped of his Saudi citizenship for criticizing the Al Saud dynasty and for suspected terrorist activities. He escaped to Sudan and then Afghanistan where, under the protection of the new Taliban leadership, he declared jihad on the American forces in the region.

The attacks were swift in coming. In 1995, a car bomb in the Saudi capital, Riyadh, killed seven people, including five U.S. servicemen. In June 1996, nineteen U.S. servicemen were killed and about four hundred people wounded when a bomb exploded at a U.S. military residence called Khobar Towers near Dhahran, a major port on the Persian Gulf.

U.S. troops were then moved to an isolated base in the Saudi desert, but their presence continued to fire up conservative opposition and create political problems for Saudi rulers. In one of his edicts in 1998, bin Laden declared, "The United States has been occupying the lands of Islam in the holiest of places, the Arabian Peninsula, plundering its riches, dictating to its rulers, humiliating its people, terrorizing its neighbors, and turning its bases in the Peninsula into a spearhead through which to fight the neighboring Muslim peoples."[6]

The Saudi rulers and the ruling clerics, however, depended on the U.S. military to keep themselves in power. They were not prepared to cut their U.S. ties because of some hotheads like bin Laden.

This calculation by the Saudi rulers and the controversy around the U.S. presence in Saudi Arabia proved fatal, as it was one of the stated motivations behind the September 11 attack on the World Trade Center.

WHAT HAPPENED TO U.S.-SAUDI RELATIONS AFTER THE 9/11 ATTACKS?

The September 11, 2001, attacks led to a wave of popular anti-Saudi sentiment in the United States and immense tension between the two governments. Despite the fact that fifteen of the nineteen hijackers were Saudi nationals, the Saudi government initially denied that Saudis played any role or that the kingdom was in any way responsible. U.S. officials insisted that Saudi education encouraged religious extremism and that Saudi money that was supposed to be going to Islamic charities often ended up in the hands of terrorist organizations.

It took several years, and Al Qaeda attacks inside Saudi Arabia itself, before the Saudis responded in earnest to U.S. pressure and began imposing controls on charitable donations and money transfers, and promised to reform their educational system. The kingdom also beefed up its cooperation with U.S. intelligence agencies.

For its part, the United States ended its official military operations in Saudi Arabia in 2003. Before that time, the U.S. Central Command's air operations for the entire Middle East was based in Saudi Arabia. In 2003, the Pentagon moved the center to Qatar and withdrew combat forces from Saudi Arabia.

MEDEA BENJAMIN

IN WHAT AREAS OF FOREIGN POLICY HAVE THE U.S. AND SAUDI GOVERNMENTS DISAGREED?

There have been many disagreements over the years. The Israel–Palestine conflict has been a source of contention from the first meeting between King Abdulaziz and President Roosevelt in 1945. The U.S. government recognized Israel in 1948 and has maintained close ties with all subsequent Israeli governments. Saudi Arabia has never had diplomatic relations with Israel.

This divergence exploded into all-out hostility in 1973 during the so-called Yom Kippur War. Syria and Egypt, with support from other Arab nations, launched a surprise attack on Israeli positions in occupied Palestinian territories. During the ensuing fight, the U.S. government sent arms to the Israelis, a move that infuriated the Arab nations. "America's complete Israel support against the Arabs makes it extremely difficult for us to continue to supply the United States with oil, or even remain friends with the United States," fumed King Faisal.[7] The Saudis joined their partners in OPEC (the Organization of Petroleum Exporting Countries) in an oil embargo against the United States and other Western states. The price of oil quadrupled by 1974 and long lines formed at filling stations.

The embargo was lifted in 1974 after the Nixon White House convinced Israel to negotiate with Syria over the Golan Heights. The crisis ended with the signing of a wide-ranging agreement between the United States and Saudi Arabia that expanded economic and military cooperation. The agreement led to the recycling of a massive amount of "petrodollars" into the U.S. economy through Saudi investments and commercial deals with U.S. companies, including military contractors.

Another area of disagreement was the 2003 U.S. invasion of Iraq. While the Saudi rulers were no friends of Saddam Hussein, they opposed the invasion. Saudi Foreign Minister Prince Saud Al Faisal called it a "colonial adventure" aimed only at gaining control of Iraq's natural resources. The Saudis were also concerned that the invasion would result in a Shia-dominated government in Iraq that would be friendly to Iran.

Despite their opposition, the Saudis did not want to anger their U.S. ally, so they secretly allowed the U.S. military to launch special operations against Iraq from Saudi air bases and granted overflight rights to U.S. planes. The Saudis also used their vast oil reserves to keep the world oil market stable during the war and continued to be the number one foreign supplier of oil to the United States.

The U.S. invasion of Iraq turned out to be one of the worst foreign policy blunders in U.S. history. Saddam Hussein was toppled, but sectarian divisions—fomented by the U.S. occupiers as part of a divide and rule strategy—led to the death of hundreds of thousands of Iraqis. And just as the Saudis had feared, Saddam Hussein was replaced by a Shia-dominated government with close ties to Iran.

The issue of how to deal with Iran has been another source of contention over the years. While Iran was a key U.S. ally under the rule of the Shah, the Islamic revolution in 1979 led to a rupture that pushed the U.S. and Saudi governments even closer together. Since then, both nations have viewed Iran as a destabilizing influence in the region. But in 2015, the Obama administration was anxious to broker a deal to ensure that Iran would not have the ability to acquire a nuclear weapon. A historic agreement was reached that limited Iran's nuclear ability in return for the lifting of international sanctions. At first the Saudi rulers opposed the deal and made noises that they would be pushed to acquire nuclear weapons to protect themselves. In the end, they reluctantly supported the Western-negotiated agreement with Iran, but they continue to be worried about a U.S. rapprochement with their main rival.

The United States and Saudi Arabia also diverged when it came to the 2011 Egyptian Arab Spring. The U.S. government reluctantly abandoned its longtime ally, President Hosni Mubarak, when it became clear that the grassroots rebellion was going to be successful; the Saudis stood by Mubarak until the bitter end. The United States tepidly supported the Muslim Brotherhood's Mohamed Morsi as the winner in Egypt's first democratic election; the Saudis opposed the Muslim Brotherhood, even though both are Sunnis. The Brotherhood's rise to power through a democratic election undermined the Saudi claim to be the legitimate leader for Sunni Islam in the region. The Saudis backed the bloody coup that overthrew Morsi and provided billions of dollars to support the new regime. The U.S. government criticized the military coup, but eventually resumed relations, including military assistance.

In Syria, the Saudis saw the uprising against President Bashar al-Assad as an opportunity to replace Assad, an Iranian ally, with a government more amenable to Saudi influence. They counted on the Obama administration to join that effort, but that hope was dashed when President Obama backed away from his 2013 threat to use direct U.S. military action against Assad's use of chemical weapons. The Saudis were furious that Obama backed down, and that he prioritized combating the Islamic State over ousting Assad. Privately, they blamed Obama for prolonging the Syrian war by stopping the Saudis from giving Syrian rebels more powerful arms, like antiaircraft missiles, because Obama feared the weapons could land in the hands of Islamic extremists.

WHAT IS THE EXTENT OF U.S. AND WESTERN WEAPONS SALES TO THE SAUDIS?

It's hard to exaggerate the enormity of Saudi weapons purchases and the key role that weapons sales have come to play in the bilateral relationship. According to a White House press release from 2014: "The Kingdom of Saudi Arabia is the largest U.S. Foreign Military Sales customer, with active and open cases valued at approximately $97 billion, as Saudi forces build capabilities across the full spectrum of regional challenges."[8] That's almost $100 billion in sales—an enormous boon to U.S. weapons manufacturers!

Most of the deals were sealed under the Obama administration. President Obama sold more advanced weaponry to Saudi

MEDEA BENJAMIN

Arabia than any of his predecessors. The 2011 deal for $60 billion constitutes the largest weapons sale to any country in U.S. history.

The weapons include F-15 fighter planes, Apache attack helicopters, missile defense systems, missiles, bombs, and armored vehicles. Weapons manufacturers such as Boeing, Raytheon, Lockheed Martin, General Dynamics, and McDonnell Douglas have been pushing these sales to offset military spending cuts in the United States and Europe. These weapons manufacturers spend millions on lobbying efforts--targeting House and Senate members who sit on the Armed Forces and Appropriations Committees—and have secured the top five largest federal government contracts since 2009.

The Obama administration has touted the Saudi weapons sales as part of a jobs program. In announcing the deal to sell eighty-four Boeing F-15s to the Saudis, for example, Assistant Secretary of State for Political-Military Affairs Andrew Shapiro boasted that the deal would create fifty thousand jobs in forty-four states. The Pentagon claims that these arms sales "improve the security of an important partner which has been and continues to be an important force for political stability in the Middle East." But the opposite is true. The weapons have been used for wars overseas that contribute to the destabilization of the region and jeopardize U.S. national security.

"Saudi Arabia's position as a strategic Gulf ally has blinded U.S. officials into approving a level and quality of arms exports that should never have been allowed to a non-democratic country with a poor human rights record," said the Federation of

American Scientists, an organization dedicated to reducing catastrophic threats to national security.[9]

The large-scale weapons sales to the Saudis have also spurred an arms race throughout the region: Israel wants to outdo the Saudis, Iran seeks countervailing weapons, and the other Gulf states compete. U.S. high-tech sales have also given the green light to other nations to sell sophisticated weapons to the region, such as Russian arms sales to Iran.

The Saudis have used U.S. weapons for putting down domestic dissent, and for quashing uprisings abroad. In 2011, the Saudi military, using U.S. tanks and weapons, rolled into neighboring Bahrain to crush the nation's budding pro-democracy movement. In 2015, the Saudis intervened in an internal conflict in Yemen, and used U.S.-manufactured fighter jets and internationally banned cluster munitions in air strikes that repeatedly hit civilian targets. More than three thousand civilians were killed, and the violence created a severe humanitarian crisis affecting 80 percent of the population. UN Secretary General Ban Ki-moon warned in January 2016 that "the use of cluster munitions in populated areas may amount to a war crime due to their indiscriminate nature."[10]

The U.S. government not only furnished the Saudis with supplies and weapons, but assisted with midair refueling, targeting information, and intelligence analysts. This intimate involvement in a war that has targeted hospitals, markets, and schools makes the United States complicit in these possible war crimes.

MEDEA BENJAMIN

During the height of the Saudi bombing in 2015, the U.S. State Department approved a new $1.29 billion sale, including over ten thousand bombs, munitions, and weapons parts produced by Boeing and Raytheon.[11] Amnesty International and other groups called on President Obama to cancel the sale since it violated the UN Arms Trade Treaty, which forbids the sale of weapons when there is knowledge the weapons will be used against civilians. "Given the evidence of how Saudi Arabia has employed such arms to date, there is overwhelming reason for concern that Saudi Arabia will use such arms to commit serious violations of international humanitarian law in Yemen," warned Michael O'Reilly from Amnesty's U.S. branch.[12]

U.S. Senators Chris Murphy and Rand Paul introduced legislation calling for restrictions on weapons sales to Saudi Arabia. "I have yet to see evidence that the civil war we're supplying and supporting in Yemen advances our national security," said Murphy, adding that U.S. military involvement was only prolonging human suffering in Yemen and "aiding the very groups that are intent on attacking us." Senator Murphy was referring to the fact that Saudi intervention in Yemen created space for the growth of both Al Qaeda and the Islamic State in Yemen.

In March 2016 in Washington, D.C., a national campaign to stop U.S. weapons sales was launched at the Saudi Summit, a gathering of Saudi scholars and activists organized by the peace group CODEPINK.

WHAT OTHER COUNTRIES SELL WEAPONS TO THE SAUDIS?

The Saudis also buy large quantities of weapons from other countries, including England, France, Germany, and Sweden, where activist groups have forced their governments to reconsider their military sales. In November 2015, responding to protests by human rights groups, UK Secretary of State Philip Hammond called for an investigation into alleged violations in Yemen, and pledged to review future weapons sales.[13] The UK government also canceled a multimillion-dollar contract to provide a training program for Saudi prison officers because of human rights concerns.[14]

In Sweden, there has been public uproar for years over Saudi military ties. In 2012, the Swedish minister of defense was forced to resign when the media leaked Swedish plans to help build a weapons factory in Saudi Arabia. In 2015, Swedish Foreign Minister Margot Wallström, who approaches foreign policy from a feminist perspective, enraged Saudi leaders and Swedish weapons manufacturers by speaking out against Saudi repression, including calling the Saudi practice of flogging "medieval." Swedish peace groups are still struggling to get their country to ban weapons sales to the Saudis.[15]

A great breakthrough in countering European arms sales to Saudi Arabia came in 2016. Following a petition signed by 750,000 European citizens calling for the suspension of weapon sales to the kingdom, the European Parliament voted to embargo weapons sales.[16] The Parliament's vote was not legally binding, but it put pressure on EU governments and reflected growing citizen involvement. Soon after that vote, the Dutch parliament passed a bill calling for the government of the Netherlands to halt weapon exports to Saudi Arabia, citing ongoing violations of humanitarian law in Yemen.[17]

WHAT OTHER MILITARY TIES DOES THE UNITED STATES HAVE WITH SAUDI ARABIA?

In addition to weapons sales, the U.S. military provides training to the Saudi military. The U.S. Military Training Mission in Saudi Arabia dates back to 1953 and was updated in a 1977 agreement to "enhance U.S. National Security through building the capability and capacity of the Saudi Arabian Armed Forces to defend our common interests in the Middle East region." The U.S. military views Saudi participation in the training program as a sound investment because it results in increased "opportunities to promote purchases of U.S. weaponry."[18]

But for many years, Congress has passed legislation banning such support to Saudi Arabia for various reasons, including its failure to adequately investigate and prevent terrorist activities. So how does the military get around these bans? Both the Bush and Obama administrations have countered these restrictions by issuing national security waivers, thereby enabling the assistance to continue.[19]

Another U.S. agency with deep ties to the Saudis is the CIA. When the CIA wants to engage in covert actions overseas without the hassle of Congressional oversight, it turns to Saudi Arabia, where there is certainly no such thing as checks and balances. Best known is the Saudi help in arming the mujahideen rebels to drive the Soviets out of Afghanistan. Lesser known is the Saudi financing of CIA operations in Angola in the 1980s, after Congress cut off CIA funds to support a brutal autocrat (Jonas Savimbi) against the Soviet-allied government. In 1984, when the Reagan administration concocted its secret plan to sell arms to Iran to finance the Contra rebels in Nicaragua, the Saudis helped out with $32 million, paid through a Cayman Islands bank account. When the Iran–Contra scandal broke and questions arose about the Saudi role, the kingdom refused to talk.[20]

The Saudis also covertly agreed to allow the CIA to operate a secret air base for unmanned drones, starting in 2011. The CIA used the Saudi base to hunt down suspected members of AQAP (Al Qaeda in the Arabian Peninsula) in Yemen. The first drone strike launched from Saudi soil was the one that killed U.S. citizen Anwar al-Awlaki. It is ironic that to quell the uproar among Saudi clerics about the U.S. military presence on Saudi soil, the Bush administration had closed U.S. bases and withdrawn U.S. forces; President Obama later came back and reopened a base.

The Saudis and Americans also share intelligence information, particularly about Al Qaeda in the Arabian Peninsula (AQAP), counterterrorism finance, the Islamic State, and the activities of Iran and Iranian-sponsored military groups. In 2010, the Saudis tipped off U.S. counterterrorism officials about bombs being shipped to the United States from Yemen in a printer cartridge.

One was found aboard a UPS plane and another on a UPS truck, and were allegedly linked to AQAP.

It is clear that the military ties reach far beyond protection for oil. The United States has become intertwined with Saudi Arabia in covert operations, and has become reliant on the regime for intelligence. It's ironic that the Saudis have made the West dependent on information about the very extremist groups the Saudis helped give birth to.

WHO PAYS FOR THE U.S. MILITARY PROTECTION OF THE SAUDI REGIME?

U.S. taxpayers are footing the bill for the U.S. military presence in the Gulf that is basically a huge subsidy for the Saudi royalty and big oil companies. There are dozens of military bases in the region, aircraft carriers, major weapons systems, personnel, and equipment, and it all adds up. By one estimate, between 1976 and 2000, the U.S. government spent over $8 trillion dollars—yes, trillion—protecting the oil flow from the Persian Gulf.[21]

In 2013, Secretary of Defense Chuck Hagel said the United States would keep thirty-five thousand military personnel in the Gulf with helicopter gunships, as well as some forty naval vessels, including an aircraft carrier battle group.[22]

Donald Trump brought this issue into the 2016 presidential race on several occasions. He said that Saudi Arabia did not properly compensate the United States for its protection. In his typically blunt tone, he said, "They make a billion dollars a day.

If it weren't for us, they wouldn't exist. They should pay us." He added, "Like it or don't like it, people have backed Saudi Arabia. What I really mind though is we back it at tremendous expense. We get nothing for it."[23]

WHAT OTHER BUSINESS TIES DOES THE UNITED STATES HAVE TO SAUDI ARABIA?

Oil remains the biggest business tie between the two countries. Saudi Arabia is the second largest source of U.S. imported oil, after Canada. In 2014, Canada accounted for 37 percent of U.S. imports, and Saudi Arabia accounted for 13 percent.[24]

Saudi state-owned oil company Aramco has major investments in the United States, including a 50 percent ownership of the largest U.S. oil refinery, which is in Port Arthur, Texas. In March 2016, Aramco announced plans to buy the other 50 percent from Shell so that it would have full control of the refinery. The Saudis could then bring more of their own crude oil into the United States for refining and selling on the U.S. market, undercutting U.S. producers.

Over the years, the Saudi government has used billions of dollars from the sale of oil to invest in commercial U.S. and European banks, and in U.S. Treasury securities. Saudi Arabia is probably the third largest investor in U.S. Treasury in the world, after China and Japan, but the exact amount is hidden from the American public. The Treasury will not disclose the Saudi holdings. It provides a detailed breakdown of the assets held by over a

MEDEA BENJAMIN

hundred other countries, but lumps Saudi holdings into a generic category of OPEC nations.

The Saudis tipped their hand, however, in 2016. In a response to pending U.S. legislation that would allow the kingdom to be sued for its participation in the 9/11 attacks, the Saudi government threatened to withdraw its money from U.S. treasury securities and other U.S. assets, which it pegged at $750 billion. Many analysts considered it a hollow threat, though, insisting that such a massive sell-off would be difficult to execute and would end up crippling the kingdom's economy. But the incident did prove how intertwined the two economies are.

There is also plenty of private Saudi money greasing the wheels of the U.S. economy, from the stock market to the real estate market. Prince Al-Waleed bin Talal, the kingdom's most famous billionaire investor, owns stakes in U.S. companies such as Citigroup and Twitter. In 2012, it was revealed that King Fahd's playboy son, Prince Abdul Aziz bin Fahd, owned $1 billion worth of U.S. real estate, from the headquarters of a television company in California to BP offices in Houston.[25]

On the other side of the equation, U.S. sales and investments in Saudi Arabia are much more limited due to Saudi government restrictions on foreign ownership and a cumbersome bureaucracy. However, U.S. contractors have entered into joint ventures with Saudi companies to help build the kingdom's vast infrastructure, including roads, commercial complexes, and communication networks, and U.S. companies exported about $35 billion in goods and services to Saudi Arabia in 2013.[26]

With plunging oil prices and renewed Saudi efforts at economic diversity, this situation is changing. In 2015, the Saudi
government offered new possibilities for foreigners to invest
in multiple sectors, including mining (phosphate, bauxite, and
silica), civil infrastructure, healthcare, retail, and banking.
Many U.S. and European banks—including Bank of America,
Morgan Stanley, and Credit Suisse—took advantage of the
opportunity to expand their operations in the kingdom. Even
the crown jewel of businesses, Saudi Aramco, is selling shares
to the public. In 2016, as part of its diversification plan dubbed
Saudi Vision 2030, the Saudis announced that they were going
to sell shares (although less than five percent) in the state-
owned oil giant. This would be the most dramatic change in the
kingdom's economic policy since the nationalization of oil in
the 1970s.

IS THERE A STRONG SAUDI LOBBY IN THE UNITED STATES?

The most powerful foreign policy lobby groups in the United
States are ones that lobby on behalf of the Israeli government.
That includes the group AIPAC (the American Israel Public Affairs
Committee), which has a massive budget of about $65 million
and a membership of over one hundred thousand supporters,
mostly in the American Jewish community.

By comparison, the Saudi lobby is new and has no grassroots
base. Its money doesn't come from members, but from the Saudi

government itself and individual, wealthy Saudis with strong ties to the government.

The Saudi government has invested heavily in improving its image by hiring high powered American public relations firms and lobbyists. They make sure to cover their bases by engaging both Democrats and Republicans, and seeking out people with influence, including former members of Congress and people who worked for key Congressional committees.

The Saudis' major investment in lobbying began right after the 9/11 attacks in 2001, when there was so much anger directed against the Saudis. The Saudi Ambassador at the time, Bandar bin Sultan, shelled out $3.2 million to the Washington, D.C.–based public relations firm Qorvis for a total makeover.[27]

Qorvis helped the Saudis publicize the part of the 9/11 Commission report that said there was no evidence the Saudi government directly funded Al Qaeda, while conveniently omitting the report's conclusion that "Saudi Arabia has been a problematic ally in combating Islamic extremism."[28] Over the years, Qorvis continuously burnished Saudi Arabia's image, including a 2015 campaign to whitewash the devastating impact of the Saudi bombing in Yemen. In its semiannual 2015 tax filing, the firm billed the Saudi Embassy for $7 million.[29]

According to *The Hill* newspaper, in 2015 the Saudis employed a total of eight American firms that performed lobbying, consulting, public relations, and legal work. After Qorvis, the next highest paid firm was the Podesta Group. This is a lobbying firm founded by top Hillary Clinton fundraiser Tony Podesta. Tony's brother and Podesta Group cofounder, John Podesta, was chair of Hillary Clinton's 2016 presidential campaign. The Podesta Group was raking in $140,000 a month from the Saudis, which would amount to $1.68 million in 2016.[30]

The law firm Hogan Lovells received $60,000 a month to set up meetings with high-ranking members of Congress. Former Republican U.S. Senator Norm Coleman, through this firm, became a registered foreign agent for the Saudi government. Prior to this, while serving in Congress in 2005, Coleman signed a congressional letter condemning the Saudi government for distributing publications that preach a "Nazi-like hatred for Jews" and for spreading extremist ideology throughout the world.[31] His public stance obviously changed when he started receiving a monthly paycheck from the Saudis.

DLA Piper was paid $50,000 a month. The Chairman of DLA Piper's Global Board was George Mitchell, whose government credentials include Senate Majority Leader and a stint as U.S. Special Middle East Envoy.

Pillsbury Winthrop Shaw Pittman got a monthly check of $15,000. The Pillsbury firm employs many former government officials, including retired U.S. Senator Saxby Chambliss, who was on both the Intelligence and Armed Services Committees.

The law firm Squire Patton Boggs is a registered foreign agent for the Saudi government. The Saudis also contracted Edelman, the largest privately owned public relations agency in the world, to represent various affiliates of the Saudi government for fees totaling $239,000. This included $190,000 to design a logo, tagline, brochures, and a promotional video for the Saudi Mission to the UN.

The eighth firm is called BGR Government Affairs, which was founded by former Republican National Committee chair Haley Barbour. It was hired in 2015 to "provide public relations and media management services" for a fee of $500,000.

This gaggle of firms meets with high-level U.S. government officials, places op-eds in newspapers, gets time on talk shows, churns out pro-Saudi propaganda, and ensures that Saudi companies get favorable treatment. Some even create the content for the Embassy's official Twitter and YouTube accounts.

For good measure, the state oil company, Saudi Aramco, contributes to several influential U.S. political groups, including the American Petroleum Institute. Thanks to the Supreme Court's Citizens United ruling, trade associations like the American Petroleum Institute can run campaign ads and get directly involved in elections. So the Saudis can now legally interfere in the U.S. electoral process.

In March 2016, the Saudis announced the launch of the Saudi American Public Relation Affairs Committee (SAPRAC), the "first Saudi public affairs organization in America." Its aim is to educate the U.S. public about the "special US-Saudi relationship," and seems to be modeled on the pro-Israel lobby AIPAC.

"Saudi Arabia is consistently one of the bigger players when it comes to foreign influence in Washington," said Josh Stewart from the Sunlight Foundation, a nonprofit group that tracks money and influence in politics. "That spans both what you'd call the inside game, which is lobbying and government relations, and the outside game, which is PR and other things that tend to reach a broader audience than just lobbying."[32]

The Saudi government has also donated to numerous think tanks, universities, and nonprofits, including the Atlantic Council, the Middle East Policy Council, the Smithsonian Freer Museum of Art, and the Arab Gulf States Institute. The Royal Embassy of Saudi Arabia and Saudi Aramco have been top sponsors of the Middle East Institute in Washington, D.C. since 2005. The Brookings Institute has received support from Aramco Services Company, the U.S.-based subsidiary of the state-owned oil company of Saudi Arabia, with donations between $25,000 and $49,999 since 2007. Aramco Services Company has also been a "premium corporate member" of the Council on Foreign Relations from 2002 to 2014, meaning that they contributed between $30,000 and $60,000 annually.

The Saudis gave between $10 million and $25 million to the Clinton Foundation. Even the Carter Center of former President Jimmy Carter, which has a major program for empowering women and girls, has taken money from a country that treats women as second-class citizens.

In 2005 Saudi Prince Al-Waleed bin Talal donated $20 million each to Harvard University and Georgetown University to "advance Islamic studies and further understanding of the Muslim World"; in 2015 a Saudi billionaire banker donated $10 million to Yale University and Yale Law School to establish a Center of Islamic Law and Civilization. Saudis also funded a center at the University of California, Berkeley.

MEDEA BENJAMIN

Lavishing money on U.S. think tanks (institutions that would not be allowed to function back in Saudi Arabia) has bought either silence about Saudi abuses or praise for Saudi "reforms" and its "stabilizing influence" in the region. In a Vox article entitled "How Saudi Arabia Captured Washington," author Max Fisher explained how it is that Washington's foreign policy community is "deeply, viscerally committed to defending and advocating for the Kingdom of Saudi Arabia, a country whose authoritarian government, ultra-conservative values, and extremist-promoting foreign policy would seem like an unusual passion project for American foreign policy professionals."[33]

He says that Saudi Arabia (and other Gulf states) started to send large checks to these think tanks and universities just when the U.S. financial crisis was taking a hefty toll on these institutions' budgets. Analysts refrained from taking contrary positions that might antagonize donors. With Saudi money pouring in, people who expressed pro-Saudi views were granted larger platforms, fatter salaries, more job security, and wider opportunities. Over time, Gulf money has distorted the lens of Washington's foreign policy community.

While D.C. firms made millions spinning Saudi policies and keeping tight relations with U.S. policymakers, they did not succeed in pulling the wool over the eyes of the American public. Despite all the lobbying, most Americans still have a dim view of Saudi Arabia. A 2014 Pew Research survey shows that 72 percent of Americans have a negative view of how the kingdom treats its citizens.[34] The same is true for the Saudis' views on U.S. policies.

It's difficult to get accurate data in a country that is so secretive and intolerant of dissenting opinions, but a rare poll taken in September 2015 showed that 81 percent of Saudi citizens had a negative view of U.S. policies.[35]

WHAT ABOUT PEOPLE-TO-PEOPLE TIES?

There is limited citizen-to-citizen exchange between Americans and Saudis. While thousands of U.S. oil and construction workers live in Saudi Arabia, they reside in Western housing compounds sealed off by high walls and gates, affording little interaction with local Saudis outside the work environment.

Saudi Arabia is one of the hardest places in the world for Americans to visit as tourists. While the kingdom opens its doors to some five million religious pilgrims a year (only during the month of Hajj to visit the religious sites through a government-sponsored travel agent), it does not issue tourist visas. Fearing cultural and political contagion, the Saudis decided to restrict travel to diplomats and businesspeople sponsored by a local business. Adding to the taboo, the U.S. State Department has issued stern travel warnings. "There have been attacks on U.S. citizens within the past year and there continue to be reports of threats against U.S. citizens. . . . Possible targets include housing compounds, hotels, restaurants, shopping areas, international schools, and other facilities where Westerners congregate," a 2015 State Department warning read.[36] Even diplomats are restricted from traveling to several parts of the country.

Saudis can, and do, travel to the United States, and many Saudi students study in U.S. universities. If there is one bright hope for better understanding, it is among the youth. According to the White House, in 2014, there were approximately eighty thousand Saudis studying in the United States.[37] These future leaders will certainly have positive exchanges with their U.S. counterparts that may foster closer people-to-people ties. These contacts are also likely to increase pressure on the Saudi regime to loosen its restrictive social mores and conventions.

SO WHAT MIGHT THE FUTURE BRING?

The U.S.–Saudi relationship has survived wars between Israelis and Arabs, oil embargoes, the Afghan war, two wars in Iraq, the 9/11 attacks, the rise of Al Qaeda, and most recently, the Syrian war and the rise of the Islamic State.

But this marriage of convenience had to be constantly justified from both sides. Saudi rulers had to convince religious zealots that the Westerners were not a threat to Saudi religious traditions; U.S. officials have had to justify the relationship as essential to U.S. national interests.

The rationale binding Western interests to the Saudi state is no longer so easily justified. "For more than half a century, Saudi leaders manipulated the United States by feeding our oil addiction, lavishing money on politicians, helping to finance American wars, and buying billions of dollars in weaponry from

U.S. companies," wrote author Stephen Kinzer. "Now the sand is beginning to shift under their feet."[38]

Maintaining dozens of bases in the Middle East at a cost of billions of dollars a year has not secured peace. Indeed, there would have been no attack on the USS *Cole* if the ship were not in Yemen, and there may never have been the 9/11 attacks if U.S. troops had not been stationed in Saudi Arabia and all over the rest of the Middle East.

And what about oil? It is certainly not necessary to have this massive military presence to protect oil supplies, especially when the United States in 2014 received only 13 percent of its oil and natural gas from the region.[39]

Moreover, this addiction to oil that is at the core of the U.S.–Saudi relationship has had catastrophic effects on the environment. Of all the negative consequences of this oil-based relationship, the worst may well be its contribution to climate change. The billions we have spent protecting the Gulf monarchies and the petrodollar system, far from increasing our security, has accelerated one of the greatest threats to our national security we have ever faced: climate chaos. If we are to have a chance at saving the planet, we have to make a transition away from a fossil-fueled economy.

So for many reasons, the U.S.–Saudi "relationship of convenience" is no longer convenient. The U.S. government and other Western nations must re-evaluate a partnership that is neither sensible, credible, justifiable, or sustainable.

CHAPTER 8: HOW THE KINGDOM RELATES TO ITS NEIGHBORS

Saudi Arabia's foreign policy is guided by several overarching and intertwined objectives: to perpetuate the House of Saud dynasty, to reduce the influence of Iran, to defend its dominance of the oil market, to promote the Wahhabi interpretation of Sunni theology, and to maintain Saudi Arabia's preeminence and influence in the region. Virtually all Saudi actions abroad can be understood through this lens.

WHAT ROLE HAS THE SAUDI MILITARY PLAYED?

Saudi Arabia spends an enormous amount of money on its military to preserve its complex objectives. Its military budget in 2016 was about $80 billion, surpassed only by the United States and China. Given its small population, it has—by far—the largest per capita military expenditure in the world. In 2015, this amounted to a jaw-dropping $6,909 per person; by comparison, the United States, with the world's largest military, spent $1,859 per person.[1]

The Saudi military, which has about 225,000 active-duty personnel, is divided into two parts: the Saudi Arabian National Guard and the regular military, which includes the Army, Air Force, Navy, Strategic Missile Force, and a Special Forces unit that has expanded in recent years to deal with terrorist attacks. Unlike in small emirates like Qatar and Bahrain, where most of the soldiers have been recruited from Pakistan or other poor countries, foreigners are not accepted in the Saudi military.

Most of the military's equipment comes from huge purchases of weapons from abroad, primarily the United States, Britain, and France. The Saudis have the most high-tech military hardware in the region, except for Israel. Their arsenal has been piling up like an oversized royal dowry, most of it going unused since the Saudis traditionally depended on the U.S. military to guarantee their security.

Some three thousand Saudi troops participated in combat against Israel during the 1948 Arab-Israeli war and another two thousand were sent to fight on the Syrian front line during the 1973 Yom Kippur War against Israel. Both times they were quickly defeated. Saudi troops helped U.S. forces during the 1991 Gulf War, but did very little of the fighting. They put down a pro-democracy uprising in neighboring Bahrain in 2011, but their opponents were unarmed, peaceful protesters. Their participation in fighting the Islamic State has mostly been in the air, where Saudi pilots have taken on some of the bombing raids.

It was really in their 2015 intervention in Yemen that the military's mettle was put to the test—and failed. Despite Saudi predictions that they would quickly defeat the ragtag Houthi army, they became bogged down in a drawn-out conflict and had to recruit troops from other countries, such as Sudan and Egypt, to do the actual fighting.

One of the major problems with the Saudi military is that the National Guard (which is not a reserve but a fully operational force of one hundred thousand and a tribal militia of twenty-five thousand) is a separate entity, not under the Ministry of Defense. It reports directly to the king and its role is to protect the royal family from internal threats. It is, by design, a superior military force capable of defeating the regular army if the army turned against the regime. Its members come from the royal family and tribes loyal to the House of Saud, institutionally tying the tribes to the monarchy. The officers are in charge of units composed mainly of their own tribal members, making the units less susceptible to outside ideas and ideologics.[2]

The military and the National Guard mistrust each other and the monarchy fears the political consequences of the two getting too close, making effective coordination difficult. This was clear during the conflict in Yemen, where the military's land force and the National Guard had command structures and communications systems that were incompatible and severely hampered coordination.

While the National Guard is considered better trained and motivated than the regular military, U.S. and British military trainers who have worked in Saudi Arabia often rate the quality of all the Saudi forces to be poor. They cite a huge gulf between officers and troops, with promotions due more to loyalty and family influence than competence. They say the military is plagued by absenteeism, and that for many, being a foot soldier is considered demeaning—all Saudis want to be fighter pilots. They are also heavily dependent on Western contractors for equipment maintenance and training.

The government's main reason for purchasing so much equipment may have more to do with politics than military strategy. Aside from the prestige of owning the brightest, shiniest planes and tanks, Saudi weapons purchases are a way to "launder" petrodollars back into Western economies.[3] This ties the West into the Saudi dynasty, allowing Saudi Arabia to escape being held accountable for spreading Wahhabism and for its own abysmal human rights record.

WHAT'S BEHIND THE SAUDI/IRAN RIVALRY?

Much of Saudi policy is determined by its long-term enmity with Iran. Saudi leaders see Iran's policies as part of an expansionist, sectarian agenda aimed at empowering Shia Muslims in the region at the expense of Sunnis. Iranian leaders attribute similarly sectarian motives to their Saudi counterparts.

It wasn't always this way. The religious division between Sunni and Shia dates back to the religion's founding in the seventh century, but Sunni and Shia have coexisted without significant conflict for much of the Middle East's history.

The Iranian Revolution in 1979 was the catalyst for deteriorating relations between the Sunni and Shia. The revolution started with a grassroots uprising in 1978 against the pro-Western, secular monarchy of Mohammad Reza Shah Pahlavi but was seized by the Islamists in 1979, who turned the nation into a Shia theocracy.

The initial message of the Iranian Islamic leader Ayatollah Ruhollah Khomeini was populist and anti-imperialist. He said Islam and hereditary monarchies were incompatible and he characterized Saudi Arabia as a U.S. agent in the Persian Gulf. Khomeini tried to position himself as the leader of all Muslims, regardless of their denomination. In doing so, he challenged the legitimacy of the Saudi royal family and called into question its status as guardian of Islam's two holy sites, Mecca and Medina. The Saudi rulers' response was to denounce Iran's revolution as an upheaval of heretical Shiites.

In essence, the Saudi–Iran split is not religious, but political. When Mohammad Reza Shah Pahlavi ruled Iran from 1941 to 1979, the Saudi government had a decent relationship with Iran, even though it was a Shiite nation. Both countries were original members of the oil cartel OPEC. The problem between them really arose when the Islamists took over Iran in 1979 and posed an ideological threat to the Saudi regime.

During the terrible Iran–Iraq war that lasted from 1980 to 1988, a war in which over five hundred thousand people died, Saudi Arabia took the side of Saddam Hussein's Iraq as a way to weaken Iran. This caused great anger among Iranians.

Relations were badly strained in 1987, when 275 Iranians died during a pilgrimage to Mecca. The Iranians had organized, as they did every year, a demonstration against the United States and Israel, and were attacked by Saudi riot police. In response, protesters in Iran occupied the Saudi Embassy and a Saudi diplomat died when he fell out of an embassy window. Saudi Arabia severed relations with Iran in 1988, and restored them in 1991.

Relations improved in the late 1990s, when Saudi Crown Prince Abdullah visited Iran and when Iranian reformist Mohammad Khatami was elected president in 2001. The 2003 U.S. invasion of Iraq, however, led to more turmoil. The power vacuum created by the overthrow of Saddam Hussein and U.S. blunders, such as firing hundreds of thousands of Sunnis in the ruling Baath Party, unleashed fierce infighting between Iraq's Sunni and Shia communities. Iran supported Iraqi Shia; Saudi Arabia supported Iraqi Sunnis.

The enmity between Saudi Arabia and Iran became even fiercer eight years later with the Arab Spring. As some regimes were toppled and others desperately clung to power, the Saudis and Iranians competed for influence and dominance. By 2016, the Saudis accused Iran of waging proxy wars in Iraq, Syria, Yemen, Bahrain, Kuwait, and even inside the kingdom itself; Iran viewed Saudi Arabia as destabilizing the entire Middle East. While some of the claims were false or exaggerated, both countries had a hand in the regional conflicts.

Another area of tension was Iran's nuclear program. The Saudis seemed to be less concerned about Iran's nuclear ambitions than the possibility that a deal would bring Iran back into the international fold and threaten the cozy U.S.–Saudi alliance. They eventually gave a nod of approval for the deal when President

Obama pledged another $1 billion in weapons sales and offered Saudi Arabia new support to defend itself against potential missile strikes, maritime threats, and cyberattacks from Iran.[4]

In September 2015, hundreds of Iranians were killed in a stampede during the annual Hajj ritual in Saudi Arabia. Tehran accused Riyadh of mismanagement, and Saudi officials accused Iran of playing politics in the aftermath of the tragedy.

Relations between the two nations came to a breaking point in 2016, when Saudi Arabia executed antigovernment activist and Shiite cleric Nimr al-Nimr on trumped-up charges of terrorism. By killing the sheikh alongside dozens of alleged Al Qaeda fighters, the Saudi government sent a clear message that it considered Shiite activists to be terrorists. The execution predictably outraged majority-Shiite Iran. After violent protests at the Saudi Embassy in Iran, Saudi Arabia cut off all diplomatic and economic ties with Tehran.

IS THE SAUDI–IRAN CONFLICT REALLY ABOUT OIL?

Some analysts contend that the Saudi–Iran split today has less to do with a religious schism that occurred over a thousand years ago or political differences and more to do with the economics of oil. Almost all of the Persian Gulf oil is located on Shia territory. Inside the kingdom, the rulers are panicked by the possibility that the Saudi Shia might secede and take their oil with them—and form an alliance with Shiite Iran. Sheikh al-Nimr had threatened to call for secession if the conditions for the Shia minority didn't improve. Saudi oil is located in the Shiite Eastern Provinces, but the royal family hoards the wealth while exploiting the Shiite workers and land. *The Intercept's* Jon Schwarz said, "If this section of eastern Saudi Arabia were to break away, the Saudi royals would just be some broke eighty-year-olds with nothing left but a lot of beard dye and Viagra prescriptions."[5]

HOW DID SAUDI ARABIA RESPOND TO THE ARAB SPRING?

The Saudi rulers were terrified by the Arab Spring that began in 2011. They viewed the determination of people in the region to overthrow undemocratic rulers as the most serious threat to the regime since the Iranian revolution.

While generally opposed to the Arab Spring uprisings, the Saudi rulers made some exceptions. In Libya, they armed the rebels to help topple Muammar Gaddafi, whom they considered a longtime adversary. This was partially due to the fact that at an Arab League meeting in 2009, Gaddafi had the gall to denounce Saudi Arabia as a creation of the British and a protectorate of the Americans. In Syria, the Saudis backed the rebels trying to overthrow Bashar al-Assad. They saw this as an opportunity to tear Syria away from Iran and integrate it back into the Arab orbit. In 2013, they became the main group financing and arming the Syrian rebels.

For the most part, however, the Saudis opposed Arab Spring uprisings and reacted by intervening militarily and financially to support friendly, autocratic governments.

MEDEA BENJAMIN

In Tunisia, the birthplace of the Arab Spring, when longtime ruler Ben Ali was toppled by the popular revolt, the Saudis offered him refuge. In Jordan and Morocco, they sent financial assistance to shore up the monarchies. In Egypt, Saudis backed the army as it crushed the country's first democratically elected government. It was in Bahrain and Yemen, however, where the Saudis played their most nefarious role.

WHAT ROLE DID SAUDI ARABIA PLAY IN CRUSHING THE PRO-DEMOCRACY UPRISING IN BAHRAIN?

In 2011, a dynamic, popular movement rose up against the repressive monarchy, the Khalifas. Headed by King Hamad, the Khalifas are the Sunni family that has ruled the country for centuries, even though the majority of Bahrainis are Shia. The protesters insisted that their revolt was not about Sunni/Shia differences but about a yearning for democratic rule.

Demonstrators set up an encampment in the central Pearl Roundabout in the capital, Manama. In this tiny country of only 1.3 million people, tens of thousands participated. The government responded with brutal force, and called on the neighboring monarchies for help.

Fearful of the example of a democratic nation on their doorstep, Saudi Arabia and the United Arab Emirates sent in their military and police forces. In March 2011, over one thousand Saudi troops and five hundred troops from the Emirates entered

Bahrain via the King Fahd Causeway. Backed by tanks and helicopters, they stormed the Pearl Roundabout, violently clearing the encampment and other protest sites.

Over one thousand protesters were arrested, including health workers treating the injured. Prisoners were beaten and tortured. Public gatherings were banned.[6] In the uprisings since 2011, some 160 people have been killed and about three thousand injured.

There continue to be demonstrations despite the ban, some numbering in the tens of thousands, but thanks to the Saudis and Emiratis, the repressive Bahraini monarchy remains in power.

WHY DID SAUDI ARABIA GET INVOLVED IN THE CIVIL WAR IN YEMEN?

Saudi Arabia has meddled incessantly in Yemeni politics since at least the 1960s. It opposed unification between the north and south in 1990, sided with southern secessionists during the 1994 civil war, and funded Wahhabi mosques and schools throughout the country.

The Arab Spring inspired Yemenis to rise up against President Ali Abdullah Saleh, who had ruled for more than three decades. Protesters railed against the lack of democratic reform, widespread corruption, and human rights abuses. Saleh yielded power to his vice president, Abd-Rabbu Mansour Hadi, who became the interim president for what was supposed to be a two-year period of social dialogue leading to new elections. When Hadi's term ended, however, he stayed in power.

MEDEA BENJAMIN

The World Bank supplied the straw that broke the camel's back in August 2014, when it pushed the interim president to suspend fuel subsidies, affecting the economic status of poor Yemeni families. The Houthis, a Shia rebel group from northern Yemen who felt marginalized and disaffected, responded by staging protests calling for the fuel subsidies to be reinstated and for a more representative form of government. The protests were met with brute force. At this juncture, the rebel movement made common cause with the deposed president Saleh and launched an aggressive military campaign in the north that later took control of the Yemeni capital, Sana'a.

President Hadi, a Sunni, fled to Saudi Arabia, where he established a government-in-exile and asked the Saudis for help. The Saudis willingly took up the fight on his behalf, intervening in what was an internal Yemeni conflict. With financial backing and air support from the Saudis, forces backing Hadi were assembled and trained to counterattack the Houthis. Saudi Arabia accused Iran of backing the Houthis financially and militarily, though Iran denied this.

The Saudis thought their bombing raids, which started in March 2015, would lead to a quick victory. But the war dragged on, causing tremendous death and suffering. By 2016, it was estimated that over twenty-eight hundred civilians had been killed, and over fourteen million of the nation's twenty-three million Yemenis had become "food insecure." Julien Harneis, UNICEF representative in Yemen, said more than a million children risked acute malnutrition. "The longer-term consequences of all this for Yemen—which was already the Middle East's poorest nation even before the conflict—can only be guessed at."[7]

Another tragic consequence of the war in Yemen is that it opened the space for two extremist groups—the Yemeni branches of Al Qaeda and the Islamic State—to flourish.

WHAT IS THE SAUDI POLICY TOWARD THE PALESTINIANS AND ISRAEL?

Saudi Arabia has long supported Palestinian rights, calling for Israeli withdrawal from the territories occupied since 1967.

The kingdom has played a role in trying to resolve the Israel–Palestine crisis and the wider Israeli–Arab conflict. In 2002, it proposed a peace plan that required Israel to withdraw to 1967 borders and to accept the creation of an independent Palestinian state, with East Jerusalem as its capital. In return, the Arab states would establish normal relations with Israel. The plan, known as the Arab Peace Initiative, won the approval of the Arab League and the Palestinian Authority, but was rejected by Israel. In 2007, the Arab League re-endorsed the initiative, which UN Secretary General Ban Ki-moon said sent a signal that "the Arabs are serious about achieving peace."[8] Once again, the plan was not accepted by Israel.

Saudi Arabia also played an active role in trying to mend the schism between the two Palestinian factions, Fatah (which controls the West Bank and East Jerusalem) and Hamas (which controls the Gaza strip). King Abdullah invited the two groups to negotiations in Mecca, resulting in the Mecca Agreement of 2007.

MEDEA BENJAMIN

The agreement soon failed and the Saudis blamed the failure on Hamas, but they continued to support a national unity government for the Palestinians.

After the 2014 Israeli invasion of Gaza that left twenty-one hundred Palestinians dead, most of them civilians, the kingdom pledged $500 million to help rebuild. Saudi's UN Ambassador Faisal al-Tarad called Israel the world's leading violator of human rights.[9]

But the Saudis continue to have a rocky relationship with Hamas for two reasons. First, Hamas has had close ties with Iran over the years (although that relationship soured when Iran backed Assad in Syria while Hamas supported the Sunni Arab rebels). Second, Hamas is an offshoot of the Muslim Brotherhood, a group the Saudis have opposed. In 2015, however, a visit by Hamas leaders to the kingdom, including a rare audience with King Salman, was seen as a warming of relations.

As for Saudi Arabia and Israel, they do not have diplomatic relations and never have. For years Saudi Arabia, along with the Arab League nations, boycotted Israeli goods. In 2005, it announced the end of its ban on Israeli goods and services, mostly to comply with its application to the World Trade Organization, where one member country cannot have a total ban on another.

Israel and Saudi Arabia do have several common positions, though: both are U.S. allies and both consider Iran an adversary.

Rumors circulated in 2015 that the two countries had been holding secret meetings and exchanging intelligence. Former Saudi and Israeli officials confirmed that the two countries had, indeed, held a series of high-level meetings to discuss shared strategic goals, particularly the growing influence of Iran in Iraq, Syria, Yemen, and Lebanon, as well as Iran's nuclear program.[10]

An Israeli representative, Shimon Shapira, who participated in some of the secret meetings with the Saudis, was quoted in a report as saying: "We discovered we have the same problems and same challenges and some of the same answers."[11]

Palestinians in the region worry that Saudi Arabia's increasingly close relationship with Israel will come at the expense of their traditional support for Palestine.

HOW HAS SAUDI ARABIA RELATED TO THE DEVELOPMENTS IN EGYPT?

The Saudi–Egyptian rivalry was one of the manifestations of the Arab Cold War dating back to the 1950s. When President Gamal Abdel Nasser came to power in Egypt in 1956, he advocated secularism, moved closer to the Soviet sphere, and insisted that Arabs should be free from Western imperialism. The Saudis, by contrast, represented monarchy and Islamist theocracy, and allied with the United Kingdom and United States.

By 1958, the relationship was so hostile that Saudi's King Saud offered a bribe to the head of Syrian intelligence to assassinate Nasser by shooting down his plane. Nasser publicly denounced the failed attempt on his life.

Relations warmed considerably in the 1970s during the presidency of Egypt's Anwar Sadat. The Saudis played a key role in persuading Sadat to expel twenty thousand Soviet military advisors from Egypt; in return, the Saudis bought the Egyptians French Mirage fighter jets to reduce Egypt's reliance on Soviet military technology. The Saudis also offered $200 million a year in aid, as well as low-interest loans.

In 1973, the Egyptian and Saudi governments coordinated the Yom Kippur War with an oil embargo against Israel's Western allies, plunging them into an economic crisis. But Egypt's relations with the Saudis soured when Egypt, against the wishes of other Arab nations, accepted the Camp David accords and made a peace deal with Israel in 1979. Furious, Saudi Arabia became one of the architects of the Arab boycott of Egypt, when seventeen Arab nations severed diplomatic ties with Cairo in 1979.

After President Sadat was assassinated in 1981, Egypt was integrated back into the Arab fold and Egyptian–Saudi ties were restored. This rapprochement also reflected a growing consensus among Gulf states that Iran had become a greater threat to them than Israel.

The Saudi monarchs had their ups and downs with the Egyptian autocrat Hosni Mubarak during his reign from 1981 until 2011, but when popular unrest forced Mubarak to step down, Saudi King Abdullah condemned the protesters and stood with Mubarak until the bitter end.

The Saudis were not happy when Muslim Brotherhood candidate Mohamed Morsi won Egypt's first democratic election in 2013. The kingdom viewed the Brotherhood as a rival center of influence in the Sunni Muslim world. When General Abdel

Fattah al-Sisi overthrew President Morsi in a military coup in 2013, King Abdullah sent a note of congratulations. While much of the world expressed outrage over the coup and the horrendous human rights abuses of the newly installed Sisi regime, the Saudis became Sisi's primary financial backer.

Saudi Arabia, along with the Emirates and Kuwait, poured $20 billion into Egypt during the two years after the coup. In return, Egypt's military joined the Saudi-led coalition fighting the Houthis in Yemen.

In April 2016, King Salman visited Egypt, praising President Sisi's iron-fisted regime and signing multibillion-dollar aid and investment deals that included a plan to build a bridge over the Red Sea connecting the two nations.

But Saudi and Egyptian foreign policy aims are not totally aligned. The Saudi rulers and al-Sisi used to have a common enemy in the Muslim Brotherhood, but in 2015, the Saudis began reaching out to the Brotherhood. Stung by what they perceived as Iran's growing influence, the Saudis wanted to strengthen the Sunni bloc against Shia Iran. They reached out to three Brotherhood-affiliated groups: Hamas from Palestine, the Tunisian Ennahda movement, and Yemeni Hizb Al-Islah.

The Egyptian regime, on the other hand, has banned the Brotherhood as a terrorist organization and puts it in the same category as Al Qaeda or the Islamic State. Egypt does not share Saudi Arabia's obsession with Iran and is more concerned about the Sunni Islamists, such as the Islamic State, who are attacking the Egyptian Sinai. These Islamists, some of whom are financed by

Saudis, are also fighting the governments of Syria and Iran. While this common adversary could pull Egypt, Iran, and Syria closer together, Egypt's financial dependence on Saudi Arabia and its close military ties will most likely keep it closer to the Saudi camp.

HOW HAVE THE SAUDIS RESPONDED TO DEVELOPMENTS IN IRAQ?

Iraq and Saudi Arabia have common interests, as they share a border of over six hundred miles. They share economic and trade interests, as well as a common history. One major difference is that Iraq is majority Shia in contrast to Saudi's Sunni majority.

The two nations had border disputes that dated back to the British carving up of territory in the 1920s. After the Iraqis overthrew their monarchy in 1958 and became a republic, the Saudis accused Iraqis of supporting covert activities against the Saudi monarchy.

Relations improved in the mid-1970s when the rulers exchanged official visits and settled outstanding disputes, such as the border issue. The 1979 Iranian revolution, which coincided with Saddam Hussein's rise to power in Iraq, gave the Saudis and Iraqis a common concern: fear that Iran would try to export its Islamic revolution. Saudi Arabia didn't want the Shiite revolution to spread and threaten its Sunni Wahhabi claim on Islam; Iraq didn't want the example of Iran to inspire a similar insurgency of the oppressed Shia population under Saddam Hussein. This fostered an unprecedented degree of cooperation between them.

Although the Saudis declared neutrality when the Iran–Iraq War began in 1980, they helped Iraq with an estimated $25 billion in low-interest loans and grants. They also reserved for Iraq part of their production from oil fields along their common border, and assisted with the construction of an oil pipeline to transport Iraqi oil across its territory.

This political alliance came to a halt when Saddam Hussein ordered Iraqi forces to invade and occupy Kuwait in 1991. Fearful that Hussein might try to take over Saudi oilfields, the kingdom supported the U.S. military intervention to repel Iraq. Saudi military bases served as the main staging areas for aerial strikes against Iraqi targets, and Saudi armed forces participated in both the bombing assaults and the ground offensive. This conflict marked the first time since its invasion of Yemen in 1934 that Saudi Arabia had fought against another Arab state.

After the Gulf War, Saudi policy focused on containing potential Iraqi threats to the kingdom and the region. Saudis supported Iraqi opposition forces that advocated the overthrow of Saddam Hussein, but they made sure to publicly denounce the 2003 U.S. invasion, even though they covertly supported the efforts. While Saddam Hussein was overthrown in 2003, it was not until 2009 that Iraq assigned its first Saudi ambassador since the Gulf War, and 2013 that Saudi assigned its first Iraqi ambassador.

The U.S. invasion and occupation destroyed the balance of power in Iraq. Shias, who had been subordinated and disadvantaged during Saddam's rule, seized power. Disenfranchised Sunnis, including some members of the Baath Party and military officers who had been fired after the U.S. occupation, took up arms.

Militias formed in both Shia and Sunni areas, and retribution became the order of the day. Many areas where Sunnis and Shia had coexisted peacefully for generations became rapidly segregated as members of each sect sought refuge. Those who did not flee risked becoming the victims of sectarian death squads. Iraq was further destabilized by the conflict in Syria, which provided space for Sunni jihadist groups to flourish.

With the Iraqi government now dominated by Shia and closely allied with Iran, relations with Saudi Arabia have soured. What remains uncertain is whether their long-term common interests will eventually override present-day conflicts.

WHAT ARE SAUDI OBJECTIVES IN SYRIA?

Syria is a majority Sunni country, but the Assad government is dominated by Alawites, a Shia-related sect that makes up less than 15 percent of the population. While the Assad family favored the Alawites as a way of keeping control, many Sunnis came to see the Alawites as willing accomplices of a brutal regime that has committed abuses against them for decades.

Peaceful uprisings against Assad were met with brutal government suppression. The country disintegrated into civil war as rebel groups and Islamic extremist groups began battling both Assad and each other. As the armed sectarian conflict continued, Iran, along with Russia and the Lebanese Hezbollah, backed

Assad; Saudi Arabia, Turkey, the United States, European nations, and Israel supported various rebel groups.

The Saudis, anxious to move Syria away from the Iranian sphere, called for the removal of Assad through force, rather than diplomacy, and for elections to install a democratic government. It was indeed ironic to hear the Saudi UN ambassador talk about the need for democratic elections in Syria when there are no such elections in the monarchy he represents.[12]

To defeat Assad, the Saudi government provided funding to the Army of Conquest, an umbrella group dominated by Syria's Al Qaeda affiliate Jabhat al-Nusra. Private funding from Gulf states provided support for other extremist Sunni groups fighting to topple Assad.

In the midst of this chaotic civil war, the Islamic State emerged. Some of the extremist groups funded with Gulf money defected to the Islamic State, taking their weapons with them. Jabhat al-Nusra is estimated to have lost about three thousand fighters to the Islamic State.

It became difficult to decipher who was fighting Assad and who was fighting the Islamic State. All nations felt threatened by the Islamic State, but they were not able to put aside their differences to focus on their common adversary.

The Saudis joined the U.S.-led coalition launching air strikes against the Islamic State starting in 2014, but its contribution was minimal. This is partly because it was bogged down in its own military intervention in Yemen and partly because it was more interested in fighting Assad. In 2015, the Saudis announced the formation of a coalition of thirty-four Islamic countries to fight terrorism, but it was unclear if it planned to focus on the Islamic State. And some "members," such as Indonesia, expressed surprise to learn through the media that they were part of the coalition.

Under pressure from U.S. officials to do more, in 2016 the Saudis offered to send troops to fight the Islamic State if the United States asked it to and if the coalition agreed to it. Many felt it was a hollow offer, given their quagmire in Yemen. Also, if Saudi troops were actually fighting on the ground against the Islamic State, they would be fighting other Sunnis, including thousands of Saudis who had joined the Islamic State. That would be very risky, inviting enormous blowback. As of 2016, the offer to send Saudi troops was simply that: an offer.

While Saudi rulers might genuinely want to defeat the Islamic State, a group that has been carrying out attacks inside the kingdom, its obsession with Iran always dominates other interests. That's why supporting anti-Shia jihadist groups in both Syria and Iraq will trump its opposition to the Sunni-based (and Wahhabi-influenced) Islamic State.

WHAT IS THE GULF COOPERATION COUNCIL (GCC) AND WHAT ROLE HAS IT PLAYED IN THE REGION?

The GCC was set up in 1981 between six Arab monarchies in the Persian Gulf: Bahrain, Kuwait, Oman, Qatar, Saudi Arabia, and the United Arab Emirates (UAE). It was formed in the wake of the 1979 Iranian revolution to collectively confront security challenges and encourage trade. It also became a forum for joint defense against Iraq after it invaded Kuwait in 1991.

Despite common interests, major political differences have arisen among its members. When the United States invaded Iraq in 2003, some states opposed the intervention while others, including Kuwait, offered their territory for use by the U.S. military.

A more long-term split has evolved regarding relations with Iran. Saudi Arabia and Bahrain have had an adversarial relationship with Iran, while Oman, Qatar, and the Emirate of Dubai view Iran as a neighbor that should be dealt with diplomatically. Oman played the role of a diplomatic bridge, hosting talks between U.S. and Iranian officials that led to the nuclear agreement.

These states not only welcomed the Iran nuclear deal but have significant economic ties with Iran. The Emirate of Dubai served as Iran's financial lifeline when international sanctions were in effect. Qatar has close economic ties with Iranian oil and gas industries. It holds regular high-level meetings with Iranian officials and generally refrains from criticizing Iran.

Another major dispute within the GCC has been between Saudi Arabia and Qatar, a tiny nation of enormous wealth thanks to natural gas. Their disagreements over the years have included a 1992 border clash that left two dead and the Saudi refusal to grant Qatar the right to build a gas pipeline through Saudi territorial waters. An even greater rift arose post–Arab Spring, when the two nations supported different sides in Egypt. Qatar supported the Muslim Brotherhood and its elected leader, President Morsi, while the Saudis supported the coup that overthrew Morsi.

Tensions extended to the airwaves. Al Jazeera and Al Arabiya are the two most viewed news stations in the Arab world; the former is funded by Qatar, the latter by the Saudis. The political differences of their backers are reflected in the TV channels. The Saudis were furious that Al Jazeera provided such detailed reporting on the bloody Rabaa massacre in 2013 that brought the coup to power and that it provided so much favorable airtime to Egyptian opponents of the coup, including the Brotherhood.

The GCC broke down into distinct political blocs over Qatar's support for the Brotherhood, with Saudi Arabia, Bahrain, and the Emirates opposing Qatar, while Oman and Kuwait remained neutral. The dispute got so bad in 2014 that Saudi Arabia, Bahrain, and the Emirates temporarily withdrew their ambassadors from Qatar.

Despite the differences, the GCC countries have deep common interests, like ensuring that their monarchies remain intact and promoting Sunni dominance in the region. In 2016, the organization was so powerful that President Obama attended their meeting in Riyadh to strengthen U.S.–GCC ties.

HOW MIGHT SAUDI POLICIES IN THE REGION EVOLVE?

There has been a dramatic increase in Saudi intervention overseas—both financially and militarily—since the time of the Arab Spring. Traditionally, the Saudis looked to the United States to intervene on their behalf in times of Middle East crises. But two factors helped change the equation: the Saudis viewed President Obama as too reluctant to intervene and King Salman's brash young son became head of the nation's military.

Saudi Arabia's unprecedented military operation against the Houthi rebels in Yemen and its participation in U.S.-led air strikes against the Islamic State in Syria are a stark departure from the nation's traditional behind-the-scenes foreign policy.

Saudi Arabia's interventionist policies, however, have come with an enormous price tag. By 2016, the Saudis were spending billions in wars in Yemen and Syria, and billions in financial aid to shore up allies in Egypt, Jordan, Morocco, Algeria, and Bahrain. This was all happening when oil prices collapsed and Saudi citizens started complaining that the government was cutting services to its own people while continuing its profligate spending abroad. Surely, the Saudi rulers will have to recalibrate.

CHAPTER 9: THE WAY FORWARD

The future of Arab nations is indeed hard to predict. While many correctly warned that the Western invasions of Iraq and Libya would lead to chaos, few predicted the Arab Spring uprisings. And who could have predicted which dictatorships would be toppled and what would replace them? So beware of facile predictions about the future of Saudi Arabia.

Some insist that the strict mechanisms of control and the conservative nature of the Saudi population guarantee that the regime will stay in place for decades to come. Others claim that just under the surface there is tremendous anger and unrest; the kingdom, they warn, is on the verge of collapse.

What is clear is that the nation is in turmoil. A key element of the turmoil is the economy. The free-fall in oil prices that began in 2014 led to a budget deficit of about 20 percent of GDP in 2015. The government has been struggling to diversify from oil and to fill in for the shrinking government sector with a more robust private sector. With great fanfare, the government announced its Saudi Vision 2030 diversification plan in 2016, but Saudi leaders have been trying for decades to wean the economy off its dependence on oil, with little to show for it. Saudi businessmen bitterly recall earlier periods of low oil prices when promises of diversification were cast aside as soon as oil prices started to climb.

More than 80 percent of government revenue still comes from oil, and while the state is trimming the budget, its spending spree on the military continues unabated.[1] In 2015, this small kingdom surpassed Russia to become the world's third largest military spender, with a defense budget of $80.8 billion.

In 2015, the International Monetary Fund (IMF) said that if present trends continued, the kingdom—once one of the most powerful economies in the world—could become bankrupt by 2020.[2] That's why Deputy Crown Prince Mohammed bin Salman announced that by 2018 at the latest, Saudi Arabia would create a massive, $2 trillion sovereign wealth fund to manage part of its oil profits and diversify its investments. This, along with spending cuts, higher taxation, and privatization of assets (including 5 percent of the oil company Aramco) are part of the royal plan.

It might work. The Saudi economy has weathered similar storms in the past, like the recession of the 1980s and 1990s, and survived intact. But this time the nation is overleveraged at home and overextended abroad.

Remember, although Arab dictators had repressed their people for decades, it was economic discontent that sparked the Arab Spring. The unspoken pact with the Saudi population is that they would tolerate the excesses of both the royal family and puritanical clerics in exchange for material comforts. A decline

MEDEA BENJAMIN

in social spending and a rise in unemployment could certainly break this pact and ignite an uprising.

A looming issue that could have a major impact on Saudi lifestyles is the climate crisis. Some analysts relate the uprising in Syria to the prolonged drought the country faced from 2006 to 2009, and the Tunisian and Egyptian uprisings to the dramatic hike in food prices resulting from extreme weather.

The Gulf nations are already experiencing some of the most extreme impacts of climate change, including "severe temperature rise, increased dust storms, sea level rise, drought and the attendant effects on both agriculture and conflict," said environmental writer Antonia Juhasz.[3]

As one of the driest countries on the planet with a rapidly growing population, Saudi Arabia has a water situation that is precarious and cannot sustain the present level of agriculture. Water-parched Saudi dairy companies have been buying up tracts of land in the American Southwest to grow alfalfa for their cows. Food prices are bound to rise as more restrictions are placed on local water consumption.

The Saudi government realizes it must also reduce domestic energy consumption, both to have more oil for export and to address the climate crisis. But Saudis are major gas and electricity guzzlers, addicted to cheap, government-subsidized energy. Fuel is sold at well under $1 a gallon and electricity for a few cents a kilowatt-hour, a fraction of U.S. prices. As a result, the roads are clogged with monster SUVs, few buildings have insulation, and air conditioners run full blast, day and night. The capital, Riyadh, is one of the most polluted cities in the world. The kingdom has only thirty million people, but is the world's sixth-largest consumer of oil. With consumption growing at nearly three times the rate of population growth, Saudi Arabia could become a net oil importer by 2038.

With this desert nation built on an unsustainable model dependent on fossil fuels and hyper-consumption, something will have to give.

IS THERE GROWING RESENTMENT AGAINST THE RULERS?

As ordinary Saudis are asked to tighten their belts, resentment toward the royal family grows. People see a nation that has squandered its wealth, with rulers living in the lap of luxury. Thousands of royals get hefty monthly stipends, and top off their income by skimming from government budgets or borrowing from banks and refusing to repay. Videos of young Saudis driving gold-plated Ferraris in Paris or having wild parties in Los Angeles mansions fuel the resentment. The wealth of the royal family is estimated at over $1.4 trillion.

Millions of Saudis see this profligate spending while in their own lives, they are faced with housing shortages, unemployment, low salaries, poor education and healthcare, and crumbling infrastructure. They see that in neighboring countries, such as Qatar and the United Arab Emirates, people have better government services and a higher standard of living.

They are upset that the government is spending billions on overseas military interventions at a time when the money is needed at home.

The resentment is particularly acute among young people. Unlike many Arab states that have declining or stable birthrates, Saudi Arabia's population is growing. While the rulers are in the geriatric crowd, more than half of the kingdom's population is under the age of twenty-five. These young people are entering the workforce in record numbers just when the economy is shrinking. They are finding it hard to get jobs, especially the cushy government jobs their predecessors were able to secure. At the same time, the cost of living is rising due to cuts in government subsidies. Many young Saudis are frustrated by the limited opportunities and doubt their government's ability to provide for their future.

The limitations are ever greater for young women. They have received an education and want to use their skills. With the rising cost of living, their desire to find employment has moved from a choice to a necessity. But when these young women attempt to take their place in the modern work environment, they are confronted with all kinds of obstacles, from a segregated workplace to the inability to even drive themselves to work.

Women are questioning the laws and customs holding them back. Millions of Saudi women travel abroad to other Arab countries, as well as to Europe and the United States. They regularly visit neighboring Oman or Bahrain for the weekend just to be able to shed their abayas and saunter freely down the streets. Many women get on the plane in Riyadh totally covered from head to toe; they remove their abayas and niqabs before landing, revealing miniskirts, tight blouses, high heels, and gobs of makeup. How must they feel when they return home to their rigid, segregated society?

Think about the women who have been educated abroad, including through King Abdullah's scholarship program that sent tens of thousands of women to universities overseas. As they studied for their undergraduate degrees, their masters, their PhDs, they had the freedom to socialize openly with men, to drive, and to dress as they pleased. They had no "male guardian" controlling their lives. How could they return home without questioning the restrictions on their freedom?

And women don't have to go abroad to see the freedoms other women enjoy. They can simply watch movies (but not in movie theaters) or TV shows from around the world. But when they venture outside their homes, they are still confronted by the meddling religious police.

Many young Saudis have expressed their discontent with their feet—they have left the country to build their lives elsewhere. In 2016, a member of the Shura Council reported that in a relatively short period of time, one million Saudis, representing 5 percent of the population, had taken up permanent residence in neighboring countries, as well as in the United States and England. He warned that the government must try to stem the flow.[4]

Add to this volatile mix another element: mounting discontent within the royal family itself. When the aging King Salman came to power in 2015, he created discord by appointing Interior Minister Mohammed bin Nayef as crown prince, making him next in line to become king, but putting his young son Mohammed bin Salman in charge of both the economy and the military. His son, who dragged the nation into the disastrous war in Yemen, is considered rash and inexperienced, and clashed with the crown prince.

But the young prince has a close relationship with his elderly father (King Salman turned eighty in 2016), and began acting as if he was the heir apparent, not bin Nayef. The power struggle between Saudi's two most powerful princes led to a broader debate within the ruling circles.

An anonymous senior prince, reportedly the grandson of the late King Abdulaziz Ibn Saud, penned a letter online, read by over two million people, calling on the thirteen surviving sons of the nation's founder Ibn Saud to unite and remove King Salman from power. "We appeal to all the sons of King Abdulaziz—from the eldest Prince Bandar to the youngest Prince Muqrin—to summon an emergency meeting with all the family to discuss the situation and do everything that is needed to save the country," the letter reportedly said.[5] Such intrigue hearkens back to 1964 when King Faisal deposed King Saud in a palace coup and calls into question the stability of the royals' inner circle.

HOW CAN SAUDI ARABIA BE TRANSFORMED?

Some Saudis believe they can make gradual reforms that will improve living conditions and open social space without really rocking the boat. They point to policies under the late King Abdullah, whom they consider a reformist. These policies include appointing women to the Shura Council, giving women the right to vote in municipal elections, and changes in the labor laws that give workers more rights. These policy changes, they contend, were the result of "soft pressure" from below; they advocate more of the same.

Others say it's a waste of time to work on these limited openings, contending that they are cosmetic at best and that many of the small gains under King Abdullah were erased when King Salman took power in 2015. The only way to make permanent gains, they say, is through structural reform.

But how? Groups of respected lawyers, academics, and professionals have long been advocating for the transformation of the kingdom from an absolute monarchy to a constitutional monarchy, where the king remains the head of state but there is an elected government that represents the citizens. Different variations of constitutional monarchies exist in about twenty-five states, from England to Japan to Morocco.

These reformists have written and gathered signatures on petition after petition, and solicited meetings with government officials to discuss their requests. One effort in 2003 called for elected regional and national parliaments within a three-year timeframe; a petition in 2011 called for women's participation in political life; another one by journalists and internet activists appealed to the youth and called for the right to form political and professional associations. Yet another called for codification of the law to limit the discretionary power of judges; legislation against sectarian, tribal, and regional discrimination; full public access to the use of public funds; a free press; and an end to indefinite detentions.

The regime has resisted every petition. When confronted with the call for a constitution, the rulers insist that the Quran is the Saudi constitution and that a human-made constitution would violate Islamic tradition. Worse yet, it responded to most of these efforts by arresting the leaders of these initiatives and throwing them in prison, along with the lawyers defending them.

The Shia minority in the Eastern Province know all too well the government's repression of nonviolent challenges to its authority. For decades Shia activists have been demanding equality and full civil rights. It was among the Shia community that the Arab Spring found an echo. Young activists began organizing protests, only to be beaten, shot, imprisoned, and tortured by government agents. The execution of the renowned nonviolent cleric Sheikh al-Nimr and other Shia prisoners in January 2016 spread fear and anger among the Shia community, and exposed the government's ironclad determination to wipe out nonviolent dissent.

The 2014 anti-terrorism laws institutionalized this crackdown, using the Islamic State attacks inside the kingdom as an excuse to criminalize practically all forms of dissent. The government's decision to treat nonviolent protest as terrorism sent a chilling message to all activists and "would-be" activists.

That is why most nonviolent activism today is either coming from Saudis in exile or has moved to the virtual sphere: the internet.

"The only way we can communicate and read each other's views is through social media," said activist Manal al-Sharif. "It's our kind of parliament, where we can go and debate, and do things we can't do in the real world."[6]

Social media is indeed one of the few spaces for people to vent. Saudis are tech-savvy, especially the youth. They may not be criticizing the government openly by protesting in public squares, but they are using Twitter, YouTube, WhatsApp, Snapchat, and Instagram to bust a hole in this otherwise closed society. Per capita, there are more smartphone users in Saudi Arabia than in the United States or Europe, and Saudis represent the Arab world's largest online population. Saudis have the highest per capita YouTube viewership in the world and generate about fifty million tweets a month![7]

Saudis are using social media to debate everything from government corruption to repressive social norms. A woman filmed her interaction with the religious police, which went viral. The vigilante told her to leave the mall because some of her hair was showing and she was wearing nail polish. The woman yelled at him to mind his own business and even called the regular police to file a complaint. "I'm putting this on Twitter and Facebook," she threatened. The video reached over 3.5 million viewers.[8]

MEDEA BENJAMIN

Human rights activists using the internet often use pseudonyms to maintain their anonymity. Others leave (or flee) the country and organize online from abroad, including internet campaigns to free the political prisoners they left behind. Ensaf Haidar, the wife of imprisoned blogger Raif Badawi, fled with her children to Canada, where she has organized an extraordinary campaign to free her husband. By 2016, he had not been freed, but the international outcry after his first fifty lashes stopped the government from carrying out the remaining 950 lashes.

While the government trawls the internet to censure and punish "hashtag activists," arbitrarily handing down long prison sentences for a tweet or a blog post, it's an impossible task to control the internet, given its ubiquitous use.

Among those who have taken advantage of this virtual opening is Sheikh Salman al-Awdah, a religious scholar with over 4.5 million followers on Twitter and several million on his YouTube broadcasts. The sheikh spent years in prison on charges of inciting rebellion against the monarchy, but he became an advocate of nonviolent change after the Arab Spring. He says democracy is the only legitimate form of government, that Islam does not permit theocracy, and that the worst despotism is that practiced in the name of religion. The government has barred Sheikh al-Awdah from print media, television, and foreign travel but he manages to stay online, perhaps because he has become "too big to jail."

Internet activism, however, goes only so far. It's an outlet for educating people and letting off steam, but it needs to be accompanied by in-person organizing. As long as security forces tightly limit political activity and social activism, the demands for change will remain frustrated. But for how long? Saudi professor Abdullah al-Hamid warned: "Without a new culture of peaceful activism, people will move underground and erupt like a volcano."[9]

The prospect of their nation "erupting like a volcano" terrifies and paralyzes many reformists. They look at the result of the political upheavals in the region and see violence and chaos. Who, they ask, would take over if the Al Saud family fell? Without political parties, independent associations, or a free media, who would fill the vacuum? The Shia in oil-rich Eastern Province might rise up to demand their independence, and take their oil with them. The military could splinter into warring factions. Al Qaeda, the Islamic State, local tribes, and any other armed groups that might emerge with the disintegration of the Saudi state could vie for power, creating a Libya-like situation. Be careful what you ask for, some Saudis warn, cautioning that the only way to avoid chaos is if change comes with the consent of the rulers.

But are the rulers capable of reform? Some members of the royal family are less conservative than the clerics and would like to see more openings (like women driving), but they know that if they go too far too fast, the conservatives will revolt.

Some see potential reformers among the clerics who are disgusted by the corruption and would like to rein in the Al Saud family. But dissent within the religious establishment is also punished by the clerics at the top, who have insisted throughout

MEDEA BENJAMIN

the decades that Muslims should obey their rulers even if they are unjust. During the Arab Spring, they issued a fatwa against demonstrating and even petition-gathering. Funded and preserved by the Al Saud family, the religious establishment is not about to bite the hand that feeds it.

The result is a closed tyrannical circle that brooks no dissent and thereby provides legitimacy to violent extremists like Al Qaeda and the Islamic State. By giving its citizens only two options—a corrupt dictatorship or violent opposition—it should come as no surprise that thousands of young Saudi men have pledged their allegiance to the Islamic State or Al Qaeda.

There needs to be a third way, something beyond the confines of tyrants and terrorists. That third way, a democratic path, would presuppose the existence of a vibrant civil society.

It would mean that instead of rotting in prison, bloggers like Raif Badawi would be free to express their opinions online. Shia youth like Ali Al-Nimr would be free to organize peaceful protests advocating for the rights of the Shia community. Women like Loujain Hathloul would be free to organize women to demand the right to drive. Lawyers like Waleed Abu al-Khair would be allowed to provide legal counsel to these activists. Professors, writers, and lawyers could come together to form groups like the Saudi Civil and Political Rights Association to put forward the types of reforms that would lead their nation down the path to democracy.

If human rights groups, women's organizations, legal collectives, and social activists were allowed to openly function, there would be an outlet for people's anger and their yearnings for participation. Gender-obsessed clerics and geriatric princes would face a lot more competition in shaping the future of their country.

WHAT COULD THE UNITED STATES AND THE WEST DO TO SUPPORT SAUDI CIVIL SOCIETY?

Year after year, the U.S. State Department puts out a Saudi country report that lays out, in excruciating detail, the "pervasive restrictions on universal rights such as freedom of expression, assembly, association, movement and religion; and a lack of equal rights for women, children and noncitizen workers." But then the government shelves the report and refuses to publicly criticize the monarchy, apply any kind of sanctions, or even restrict weapons sales.

In a fascinating 2016 interview with President Obama by journalist Jeffrey Goldberg, Obama criticized the Saudi rulers for everything from state-sanctioned misogyny and spreading an intolerant interpretation of Islam to their refusal to "share" the Middle East with their Iranian foes.[10]

Most telling of all, Goldberg said that Obama was "clearly irritated that foreign-policy orthodoxy compels him to treat Saudi Arabia as an ally." How remarkable that the U.S. president, the most powerful man in the world, felt hemmed in by a Cold War–era alliance that no longer serves the interests of the United States, if it ever did.

MEDEA BENJAMIN

It's time to break with that orthodoxy and reexamine the basic assumptions about that alliance.

1. **Assumption: We need stable allies in the region and Saudi Arabia is one of the very few.**

   For many decades, the U.S. government has viewed the Saudis as a rock of stability in a volatile region. Perhaps that was the case many years ago (with U.S. military backing, of course), but it is certainly not true today. Saudi Arabia is responsible for much of the chaos in the region, and the kingdom itself could erupt like a volcano at any moment.

2. **Assumption: We need Saudi oil for our energy needs.**

   The United States gets only 13 percent of its oil from Saudi Arabia, and there is a glut of oil in the global market. U.S. domestic production and increased supplies from non-Arab countries, along with green-energy alternatives and better conservation/efficiency, reduce Saudi leverage. And one day Saudi oil will run out. Gone are the days when the Saudis could use their oil to hold the U.S. hostage. Today, it is the Saudis who are held hostage by their own dependence on oil revenues.

3. **Assumption: We need Saudi intelligence cooperation to stop terrorist attacks against us.**

   Years of Saudi intelligence cooperation certainly didn't stop the 9/11 attacks. Today, the Saudis offer intelligence-sharing and token assistance in fighting the Islamic State, but they bear great responsibility for creating the very groups they are giving us intel about. Besides, if the U.S. government didn't help prop up this unelected, despotic regime (and didn't have military on Saudi soil in the first place), the United States would be less of a target for terrorist attacks.

It's shameful that for decades the U.S. government and its Western allies have been supporting Saudi kings, princes, and religious fanatics. It's shameful that the U.S. government has authorized the sale of billions of dollars of weapons to a regime that beheads peaceful protesters and bombs civilians in neighboring nations. The U.S. government should ban weapons sales to the kingdom, as some of our counterparts in Europe are doing. Instead of state visits and trade deals and "best friends forever" status, the U.S. relationship should be conditioned on democratic openings.

Our real Saudi allies should be the human rights leaders, the pro-democracy advocates, the lawyers calling for a fair legal system, the migrant workers demanding their rights, the women trying to overturn the guardianship system, and the religious minorities asking for full citizenship. These are the groups and individuals who deserve our support, our friendship, and our admiration. These are the people who can build a modern nation that respects and protects the rights of all its inhabitants.

Credit: Gregory Johnson of Resources for Life. http://www.resourcesforlife
.com/docs/item10204/20150119tu-diplomacy-us-president-george-w-
bush-holds-hand-with-king-saudi-arabia-6446422

Prominent Shia cleric Sheikh al-Nimr, who was executed in January 2016 for his criticism of the Saudi regime.

Photo courtesy of Mustafa al-Nimr.

A home in Sanaa, Yemen is destroyed by the Saudi airstrikes that began in March 2015.

Image captured by Ibrahem Qasim, 13 June 2015. Available on Wikipedia, "Destroyed House in the South of Sanaa." https://commons .wikimedia.org/wiki/File:Destroyed_house_in_the_south_of_Sanaa_ 12-6-2015-3.jpg (No changes made)

The government of Saudi Arabia cracks down on dissent, and censors a vast range of media and online sources.

Cartoon by Carlos Latuff, March 31 2013. Available on Latuff Cartoons, "Saudi Arabia May Block Messaging Apps." https://latuffcartoons.wordpress.com/tag/saudi-arabia/

Thousands of protesters gather around the Pearl Roundabout in February 2011 in Bahrain to demand basic rights, just days before the before Saudi tanks rolled in to crush peaceful protesters.

ACKNOWLEDGMENTS

I give deep gratitude to my Saudi friends who helped me gain some understanding of their complicated country. Unfortunately, many of them cannot be publicly acknowledged for their own safety. I am indebted to Marwa Al-Faraj, who has not only been a wonderful reader and fact-checker, but a great friend. You give me great hope for the future of Saudi women. Another Saudi I truly admire is Ali al-Ahmed, director of the D.C.-based Gulf Institute. Ali has publicly challenged the Saudi regime since the time he was put in prison at age fourteen. He is one of the bravest people I know and without him, CODEPINK would never have joined the ranks of Saudi dissidents—protesting outside the D.C. Embassy, crashing U.S.–Saudi business events, speaking out at Congressional hearings. Thank you, Ali, for your decades of struggle, all too often in the wilderness.

I feel blessed to have the support of my CODEPINK sisters, who make this work so rewarding. Rebecca Green has been a tremendous assistant, giving terrific feedback and filling in hundreds of footnotes, and Crystal Zevon was so helpful in disentangling the pieces when I got stuck. I appreciate the constant

MEDEA BENJAMIN

encouragement from CODEPINK cofounder Jodie Evans and my colleagues Alli McCracken, Janet Weil, Ann Wright, Nancy Kricorian, Nancy Mancias, Farida Sharalam, Chelsea Byers, Sam Ritchie, Ariel Gold, and Alice Newberry.

Sandy Davies and Michael Eisenscher provided wonderful research help, and I appreciate the feedback from Ali Moosvi, Stanley Heller, Judy Bello, Marguerite Rosenthal, Lenni Brenner, Hala Aldosari, Kristine Beckerle, and Joe Lombardo.

Many thanks to OR Books publisher John Oakes and the wonderful crew at OR, particularly Justin Humphries and Jen Overstreet, for their work and encouragement.

Finally, I want to thank my partner Tighe Barry for traveling with me on numerous and sometimes dangerous trips to the Middle East, for tolerating the late-night dates with my computer, for his companionship and love. I also owe a debt of gratitude to my children, Arlen and Maya, and my granddaughter Chemina, for motivating me to leave a better world for them.

GLOSSARY FOR ARABIC TERMS
USED IN *KINGDOM OF THE UNJUST*

Abaya: A thick, opaque, and loose-fitting cloak that conceals the shape of women's bodies. It covers all but women's hands and face, and it is usually used along with the hijab, or headscarf. By law, women in Saudi Arabia are required to wear abayas in public spaces over their everyday clothing.

Alawite: A Shia-related branch of Islam that is centered in Syria. Despite constituting only 10 to 15 percent of the Syrian population, the Alawites dominate the Assad government.

Burqini: Abaya-like swimwear that most women in Saudi Arabia are required to wear if they choose to go swimming.

Fatwa: In the Islamic faith, the term refers to the legal opinion that a jurist or mufti can give on issues pertaining to Islamic law.

Grand Mufti: The highest official of religious law in a Sunni Muslim country.

Hafiz: Saudi Arabia's unemployment benefits program.

Hajj: An annual Islamic pilgrimage to the holy site of Mecca, Saudi Arabia, which is a mandatory religious duty for Muslims that must

MEDEA BENJAMIN

be carried out at least once in their lifetime by all who are physically and financially capable. The Hajj is annually the largest gathering of people anywhere in the world.

Hay'ai The Committee for the Promotion of Virtue and the Elimination of Vice, also referred to as the Mutaween ("the pious") or the religious police. The hay'a patrol the streets in Saudi Arabia enforcing the strict Wahhabist interpretation of Sharia, such as dress codes, the strict separation of unrelated men and women, the ban on alcohol, and the observance of prayer.

Hijab: The veil or headscarf that covers the head and chest, which is worn by some Muslim women beyond the age of puberty in the presence of adult males outside of their immediate family and non-Muslims.

Hudud: A section of Sharia law that deals with serious crimes.

Hussainiyya: Shia prayer halls that commemorate the martyrdom of Imam Husayn, the third Shia Imam. In Shia areas around the world, these houses are like community centers, used for religious rituals, praying, social gatherings, and weddings.

Iqama: A residency permit that allows foreign workers to gain employment in Saudi Arabia. This must be issued through a legal resident or Saudi national, who then becomes the foreign worker's legal sponsor.

Jihad: An Islamic term meaning "striving" or "struggling" to be a better Muslim or spread Islam. Despite Western interpretation, military action is only one means of waging jihad, and is very rare.

Kafala: A system in Saudi Arabia that ties the residency status of migrant workers to their employers, granting the latter total control. Human rights groups call this system a form of indentured servitude.

Kafeel: A legal resident or Saudi national who serves as a sponsor to a foreign worker under the kafala system.

Madrassa: The Arabic word for "school."

Majiis Al-Shura: Also known as the Shura Council, the Majiis Al-Shura is a consultative body of 150 members appointed by the king for four-year terms that can be renewed. The Shura Council can propose legislation but has no legislative powers.

Mawlids: The Sufi celebrations of the birth and life of Muhammad.

Mujahideen: The armed resistance fighters in Afghanistan who were funded by the CIA and the Saudis to fight the Soviet occupation in the 1980s. From the funding and arming of the Mujahideen emerged the Taliban, and later Al Qaeda. Mujahideen translates to "holy warriors."

Mutaween: The Committee for the Promotion of Virtue and the Elimination of Vice, also referred to as hay'a or the religious police. They patrol the streets enforcing the Saudi interpretation of Sharia, such as dress codes, the strict separation of unrelated men and women, the ban on alcohol, and the observance of prayer. Mutaween means "the pious" in Arabic.

Niqab: A face veil worn by some Muslim women that covers everything except for the eyes.

Nitaqat: A government program implemented in 2000 as part of a policy of "Saudization," which mandated that businesses with more than twenty employees must employ at least 25 percent Saudis.

Sharia: The religious legal system governing the members of the Islamic faith. Sharia is the official state law in Saudi Arabia.

Shia: Shia is a branch of Islam whose followers believe that the Prophet Muhammad's proper successor as caliph was his son-in-law and cousin Ali ibn Abi Talib. Saudi Arabia is a majority Sunni country, with only 10 to 15 percent Shia.

Shiaat Ali: Shiaat Ali translates to "the partisans of Ali." The Shia sect draws its name from this phrase, as it was around their belief that Ali ibn Abi Talib should be the Prophet Muhammad's successor that they became an independent branch of Islam.

Sufism: A practice of Islam that can be exercised by Shia or Sunni. Sufism is spiritual and mystic, characterized by its use of music, dance, meditation, and the teachings of Sufi masters.

Sunni: Sunni is a branch of Islam whose followers believe that the Islamic Prophet Muhammad's proper successor as caliph was Muhammad's father-in-law Abu Bakr. Saudi Arabia is a majority Sunni country.

Sunnah: The verbally transmitted record of the traditions and practices of the Prophet Muhammad.

Talib: The Arabic word for "student." The Taliban derived their name from the word *talib*, as they had their origins in Saudi-funded schools in Pakistan that taught Wahhabist ideology in the 1980s.

Thobe: Traditional white Arabian robes that men often wear in Saudi Arabia.

Ulema: Religious leaders in Saudi Arabia. The ulema has a direct role in government, from approving the king and royal decrees to enforcing the nation's moral and social rules.

Wahhabism: The austere form of Sunni Islam that comes from the teachings of eighteenth-century religious scholar Muhammed ibn Abd al-Wahhab.

Wali: A legally recognized male guardian who supervises a woman, no matter her age. A wali must be a woman's father, husband, uncle, or other male relative (even her son), and must grant formal permission for most of the significant issues affecting her life.

Zakat: An Islamic religious obligation in which individuals and companies donate 2.5 percent of their income to charity.

FURTHER RESOURCES

CAMPAIGNS

The following groups have campaigns involved in one or more of the following issues: ending the sale of weapons; supporting human rights activists, political prisoners, and journalists; advocating for the rights of women, migrant workers, religious minorities, and journalists. If you have other groups we should add to this list, or any comments or suggestions, please send them to us at info@codepink.org.

I hope you will go to the CODEPINK website to sign up for our weekly alerts. We look forward to staying in touch with you and working together to support the courageous Saudi activists, and stop our governments from defending the Saudi regime.

CODEPINK (Los Angeles and Washington, D.C.)
www.codepink.org

The Institute for Gulf Affairs (Washington, D.C.)
www.gulfinstitute.org

End the U.S–Saudi Alliance
www.saudius.org

Amnesty International (London and New York)
www.amnesty.org
www.amnestyusa.org

Human Rights Watch (New York)
www.hrw.org

Avaaz
www.avaaz.org

Reprieve (London)
www.reprieve.org.uk

Campaign Against Arms Trade (London)
www.caat.org.uk

Project Ploughshares (Waterloo, Canada)
ploughshares.ca

European Saudi Organization for Human Rights (Berlin)
www.esohr.org
www.esohr.org/en

RESOURCES

Aarts, Paul, and Carolien Roelants. *Saudi Arabia: Kingdom in Peril.* London: C. Hurst & Co., 2015.

Abukhalil, As'Ad. *The Battle for Saudi Arabia: Royalty, Fundamentalism and Global Power.* New York: Seven Stories Press, 2004.

Al-Rasheed, Madawi. *A Most Masculine State: Gender, Politics and Religion in Saudi Arabia.* Cambridge University Press, 2013.

Al-Rasheed, Madawi. *Muted Modernists.* London: C. Hurst & Co., 2015.

Bronson, Rachel. *Thicker Than Oil: America's Uneasy Partnership with Saudi Arabia.* Oxford University Press, 2006.

Commins, David. *The Wahhabi Mission and Saudi Arabia.* New York: I. B. Tauris & Co., 2009.

Cooper, Andrew Scott. *The Oil Kings: How the U.S., Iran, and Saudi Arabia Changed the Balance of Power in the Middle East.* New York: Simon & Schuster, 2011.

House, Karen Elliott. *On Saudi Arabia: Its People, Past, Religion, Fault Lines—and Future.* Vintage Books, 2012.

Jones, Toby Craig. *Desert Kingdom: How Oil and Water Forged Modern Saudi Arabia.* President and Fellows of Harvard College, 2010.

Kosebalaban, Hasan, and Mohammed Ayoob. *Religion and Politics in Saudi Arabia: Wahhabism and the State.* Lynne Rienner, 2009.

Mabon, Simon. *Saudi Arabia and Iran, Soft Power Rivalry in the Middle East.* New York: I. B. Tauris & Co., 2013.

Matthiesen, Toby. *The Other Saudis: Shiism, Dissent, and Sectarianism.* Cambridge University Press, 2015.

Valentine, Simon Ross. *Force and Fanaticism: Wahhabism in Saudi Arabia and Beyond.* London: C. Hurst & Co., 2015.

DOCUMENTARIES/FILMS

Saudi Arabia Uncovered, PBS *Frontline*
http://www.pbs.org/wgbh/frontline/film/saudi-arabia-uncovered/

Saudi's Secret Uprising, BBC News
http://www.bbc.com/news/world-middle-east-31915367

Wadjda, feature film by Saudi female director Haifaa al-Mansour
http://www.imdb.com/title/tt2258858/

The Real House of Saud, Empire Files
http://topdocumentaryfilms.com/real-house-saud/

OTHER RESOURCES

Middle East Eye
middleeasteye.net

Al-Monitor
al-monitor.com

Al Arabiya
https://english.alarabiya.net/

ENDNOTES

CHAPTER 1

1. Toby Craig Jones. *Desert Kingdom: How Oil and Water Forged Modern Saudi Arabia.* Cambridge, MA: Harvard UP, 2010. Print.
2. "Saudi Arabia." *Energy Information Administration.* 2015. https://www.eia.gov/beta/international/country.cfm?iso=SAU.
3. Javier Blas, "Too Big to Value: Why Saudi Aramco is in a League of its Own." Bloomberg News. 7 January 2016. http://www.bloomberg.com/news/articles/2016-01-07/too-big-to-value-why-saudi-aramco-is-in-a-league-of-its-own.
4. David Leigh and Rob Evans. "Blair Called for BAE Inquiry to be Halted." *The Guardian.* 22 December 2007. http://www.theguardian.com/baefiles/story/0,,2231496,00.html.
5. "Underground Party Scene in Jeddah: Saudi Youth Frolic Under 'Princely Protection.'" *WikiLeaks.* 18 November 2009. https://wikileaks.org/plusd/cables/09JEDDAH443_a.html.
6. Ben Hubbard. "Saudi King Unleashes a Torrent of Money as Bonuses Flow to the Masses." *International New York Times.* 19 February, 2015. http://www.nytimes.com/2015/02/20/world/middleeast/saudi-king-unleashes-a-torrent-as-bonuses-flow-to-the-masses.html.

7. Julia Glum. "Saudi Arabia's Youth Unemployment Problem Among King Salman's Many New Challenges After Abdullah's Death." *International Business Times.* 23 January 2015. http://www .ibtimes.com/saudi-arabias-youth-unemployment-problem-among-king-salmans-many-new-challenges-after-1793346.

8. Aryn Baker. "Rich Nation, Poor People: Saudi Arabia." *Time* magazine. 23 May 2013. http://time.com/3679537/ rich-nation-poor-people-saudi-arabia/.

9. *Saudi's Secret Uprising.* BBC News. 16 March 2015. http://www.bbc. com/news/world-middle-east-31915367.

10. Hubbard, "Saudi King Unleashes a Torrent of Money as Bonuses Flow to the Masses." http://www.nytimes.com/2015/02/20/ world/middleeast/saudi-king-unleashes-a-torrent-as-bonuses-flow-to-the-masses.html.

11. Daisy Carrington. "Twitter Campaign Highlights Poverty in Saudi Arabia." *Inside the Middle East.* 6 September 2013. Web. http://www.cnn.com/2013/09/05/world/meast/twitter-campaign-highlights-poverty/.

12. Ben Moshinsky. "Saudi Arabia Spends 25% of its Budget on its Military—Here's What it has for the Money." *Business Insider.* 31 December 2015. Web. http://www.businessinsider.com/saudi-arabia-spends-25-of-its-budget-on-its-military-2015-12?r=UK&IR=T.

13. *Commission for the Promotion of Virtue and the Prevention of Vice.* Washington: Americans for Democracy & Human Rights in Bahrain, 2015. Web. http://www.adhrb.org/wp-content/ uploads/2015/04/2015.03.31_Ch.-1-CPVPV.pdf.

14. Andrew Hammond. *The Islamic Utopia: The Illusion of Reform in Saudi Arabia.* London: Pluto Press, 2012.

15. Mustafa Hameed. "The Destruction of Mecca: How Saudi Arabia's Construction Rampage Is Threatening Islam's Holiest City." *Foreign*

Policy. 22 September 2015. Web. http://foreignpolicy.com/2015/09/22/the-destruction-of-mecca-saudi-arabia-construction/.

16. Carla Power. "Saudi Arabia Bulldozes Over Its Heritage," *Time* magazine. 14 November 2014, http://time.com/3584585/saudi-arabia-bulldozes-over-its-heritage/.

17. Fatima Ghani, Michael Lipka. "5 Facts About the Hajj." Pew Research Center. 11 October 2013. Web. http://www.pewresearch.org/fact-tank/2013/10/11/5-facts-about-the-hajj/.

CHAPTER 2

1. U. S. Commission on International Religious Freedom. *2013 Annual Report.* 113th Congress. Washington, D.C.: 2013. PDF file. http://www.uscirf.gov/sites/default/files/resources/2013%20USCIRF%20Annual%20Report%20(2).pdf.

2. Abdullah bin Abdulaziz Al Saud. *Saudi King Abdullah Talks to Barbara Walters.* ABC News, 2005. Web. http://abcnews.go.com/2020/International/story?id=1214706.

3. United States Bureau of Democracy, Human Rights, and Labor. *International Religious Freedom Report 2004.* 108th Congress. Washington, D.C.: 2004. Web. http://www.state.gov/j/drl/rls/irf/2004/35507.htm.

4. Richard Spencer. "Saudi Arabia Court Gives Death Penalty to Man Who Renounced His Muslim Faith." *The Telegraph,* 24 February 2015. Web. http://www.telegraph.co.uk/news/worldnews/middleeast/saudiarabia/11431509/Saudi-Arabia-court-gives-death-penalty-to-man-who-renounced-his-Muslim-faith.html.

5. Faiza Saleh Ambah. "In Saudi Arabia, a Resurgence of Sufism." *The Washington Post.* 2 May 2006. Web. http://www.washingtonpost.com/wp-dyn/content/article/2006/05/01/AR2006050101380.html.

6. "Saudi Arabia: Treat Shia Equally." *Human Rights Watch*, 3 September 2009. Web. https://www.hrw.org/news/2009/09/03/saudi-arabia-treat-shia-equally.

7. Madawi al-Rasheed. *Saudi Arabia's Domestic Sectarian Politics.* Norwegian Peacebuilding Resource Centre Policy Brief. August 2013.

8. Anonymous for personal safety. Personal interview with Saudi woman. Washington, D.C., 18 February 2016.

9. Rasheed. "Islam in Saudi Arabia." *Bible Discovered*, 18 January 2009. Web. http://www.biblediscovered.com/islamic-revolutions/islam-in-saudi-arabia/.

10. Frederic Wehrey. *The Forgotten Uprising in Eastern Saudi Arabia.* Washington, D.C.: Carnegie Endowment for International Peace, 2013. PDF file.

11. Amnesty International. *Saudi Arabia: Detention without Trial of Suspected Political Opponents.* 1990. PDF file.

12. Matt Hadro. "Religious Freedom Group Condemns Saudi Arabia's Execution of Shi'a Cleric." *Catholic News Agency*, EWTN Global Catholic Network, 6 January 2016. Web. http://www.catholicnewsagency.com/news/religious-freedom-group-condemns-saudi-arabias-execution-of-shia-cleric-82457/.

13. United States. Congress. House of Representatives. *International Religious Freedom Act of 1998.* 27 January 1998. PDF file. http://www.state.gov/documents/organization/2297.pdf.

14. U. S. Commission on International Religious Freedom. *2013 Annual Report.* http://www.uscirf.gov/sites/default/files/resources/2013%20USCIRF%20Annual%20Report%20(2).pdf.

CHAPTER 3

1. Freedom House. "Freedom in the World: Saudi Arabia." 2016, Web. https://www.freedomhouse.org/report/freedom-world/2014/saudi-arabia.

2. Jay Nordlinger. "A Saudi Woman Struggles for Her Husband, a Political Prisoner." *National Review.* 8 March 2016. Web. http://www.nationalreview.com/article/432454/saudi-political-prisoner-raif-badawi-and-his-wife-ensaf-haidar.

3. "Saudi Arabia Convicts TV Presenter for Critical Show." *Committee to Protect Journalists.* 6 February 2014. Web. https://cpj.org/2014/02/saudi-arabia-convicts-tv-presenter-for-critical-sh.php.

4. "Saudi Arabia: Long Prison Terms for Activists." *Human Rights Watch.* 27 October 2015. Web. https://www.hrw.org/news/2015/10/27/saudi-arabia-long-prison-terms-activists.

5. Ibrahim Nafie. "How Do We Report Our Friends? Saudi Managers of 'WhatsApp' Comment on the Law That Threatens Them with Imprisonment." *Huffington Post.* 7 January 2016. http://www.huffpostarabi.com/2016/01/07/story_n_8932420.html.

6. James Jones. *Saudi Arabia Uncovered.* Film. PBS Frontline, 29 March 2016. http://www.pbs.org/wgbh/frontline/film/saudi-arabia-uncovered/.

7. Adam Coogle. "Dispatches: Saudi Arabia's Unrelenting Assault on Free Expression." *Human Rights Watch.* 7 May 2014. https://www.hrw.org/news/2014/05/07/dispatches-saudi-arabias-unrelenting-assault-free-expression.

8. "Saudi Arabia Put in Charge of Human Rights Panel." Reporters Without Borders. 21 September 2015. Web. http://en.rsf.org/saudi-arabia-saudi-arabia-put-in-charge-of-21-09-2015,48377.html.

9. "Muzzling Dissent: Saudi Arabia's Efforts to Choke Civil Society." *Amnesty International.* 9 October 2014. Web. https://www.amnesty.org/en/press-releases/2014/10/muzzling-dissent-saudi-arabia-s-efforts-choke-civil-society/.

10. Adam Coogle. "The Price of Standing Up for Rights in Saudi Arabia." *Human Rights Watch.* 15 January 2015. Web. https://www.hrw.org/news/2015/01/15/price-standing-rights-saudi-arabia.

11. "NGO Law Monitor: Saudi Arabia." *The International Center for Not-for-Profit Law.* 12 December 2015. Web. http://www.icnl.org/research/monitor/saudiarabia.html.

12. Sharan Burrow. *The 2015 ITUC Global Rights Index: The World's Worst Countries for Workers.* International Trade Union Confederation, 2015. Web. http://www.ituc-csi.org/IMG/pdf/survey_global_rights_index_2015_en.pdf.

13. "Saudi Arabia: Terrorism Law Tramples on Rights." *Human Rights Watch.* 6 February 2014. Web. https://www.hrw.org/news/2014/02/06/saudi-arabia-terrorism-law-tramples-rights.

14. "I Would Have Confessed to Anything." *The Guardian.* 9 May 2005. Web. http://www.theguardian.com/world/2005/may/10/alqaida.saudiarabia.

15. "Saudi Arabia: Public Flogging of Blogger 'Cruel and Inhuman,' Says UN Rights Chief." *UN News Centre.* 15 January 2015. Web. http://www.un.org/apps/news/story.asp?NewsID=49809#.VuHj23QrIzA.

16. Francois Lenoir. "The World's Most Barbaric Punishments." *Newsweek.* 8 July 2010. Web. http://www.newsweek.com/worlds-most-barbaric-punishments-74537.

17. "The Death Penalty in Saudi Arabia: Facts and Figures." *Amnesty International.* 25 August 2015. https://www.amnesty.org/en/latest/news/2015/08/the-death-penalty-in-saudi-arabia-facts-and-figures/.

18. "Saudi Arabia: Surge in Executions." *Human Rights Watch.* 21 August 2014. Web. https://www.hrw.org/news/2014/08/21/saudi-arabia-surge-executions.
19. "Saudi Arabia: Little Rights Progress Under King Salman." *Human Rights Watch.* 3 September 2015. Web. https://www.hrw.org/news/2015/09/03/saudi-arabia-little-rights-progress-under-king-salman.
20. Nick Robins-Early. "Saudi Arabia Ends a Brutal Year of Executions by Beheading a Filipino National." *The World Post.* 31 December 2015. Web. http://www.huffingtonpost.com/entry/saudi-arabia-executions-zapanta_us_5684096cc4b014efe0d9bfdf.
21. "Saudi Arabia: Fears Grow That Three Young Activists Could Soon Be Executed." *Amnesty International.* 16 October 2015 https://www.amnesty.org/en/latest/news/2015/10/saudi-arabia-three-young-activists-could-soon-be-executed/.
22. Julianne Hill. Speech at Saudi summit, 5 March 2016.
23. Anonymous. Personal interview with Saudi woman. Washington, D.C., 2 March 2016.
24. Nadya Labi, "The Kingdom in the Closet." *The Atlantic.* May 2007. http://www.theatlantic.com/magazine/archive/2007/05/the-kingdom-in-the-closet/305774/.
25. "Three US Women Claim Sexual Assault by Saudi Prince in Beverly Hills Mansion." *The Guardian.* 27 October 2015. http://www.theguardian.com/us-news/2015/oct/27/saudi-arabia-prince-american-women-sexual-assault-beverly-hills.
26. Lora Moftah. "'Gay Parties' Raided in Saudi Arabia; Religious Police Arrest Several People on Suspicion of Homosexuality." *International Business Times.* 15 June 2015. Web. http://www.ibtimes.com/gay-parties-raided-saudi-arabia-religious-police-arrest-several-people-suspicion-1968038.

27. Jeremy Diamond. "Obama Defends Saudi Relationship: 'Sometimes We Have to Balance.'" *CNN.* 27 January 2015. Web. http://www.cnn.com/2015/01/27/politics/obama-saudi-arabia-zakaria/.
28. Owen Bowcott. "UK and Saudi Arabia 'in Secret Deal' Over Human Rights Council Place." *The Guardian.* 29 September 2015. http://www.theguardian.com/uk-news/2015/sep/29/uk-and-saudi-arabia-in-secret-deal-over-human-rights-council-place.
29. "Again: Saudi Arabia Elected Chair of UN Human Rights Council Panel." *UN Watch.* 20 September 2015. http://www.unwatch.org/again-saudis-elected-chair-of-un-human-rights-council-panel/.
30. "Muzzling Dissent: Saudi Arabia's Efforts to Choke Civil Society." *Amnesty International.* 9 October 2014. Web. https://www.amnesty.org/en/latest/news/2014/10/muzzling-dissent-saudi-arabia-s-efforts-choke-civil-society/.

CHAPTER 4

1. Saudiwoman. "Opposition to a Saudi White Ribbon Campaign." *Saudiwoman's Weblog.* 21 May 2013. Web. https://saudiwoman.me/2013/05/21/opposition-to-a-saudi-white-ribbon-campaign/.
2. Ebtihal Mubarak. Speech at Saudi Summit, Washington, D.C. 5 March , 2016.
3. Susie of Arabia. "On Gender Equality." *Susie of Arabia.* 9 November 2015. Web. http://susiesbigadventure.blogspot.com/2015/11/on-gender-equality.html.
4. "Statistics: Saudi Arabia." *UNICEF.* 27 December 2013. Web. http://www.unicef.org/infobycountry/saudiarabia_statistics.html.
5. Roula Baki. "Gender-Segregated Education in Saudi Arabia: Its Impact on Social Norms and the Saudi Labor Market." *Education*

Policy Analysis Archives Journal 12 (2004): 28. *Web.* http://epaa.asu. edu/ojs/article/viewFile/183/309.

6. Cynthia Miley. "Saudi Arabia Permits First Women Lawyers to Practice Law." *Jurist.* 7 October 2013. Web. http://jurist.org/ paperchase/2013/10/saudi-arabia-permits-first women-lawyers- to-practice-law.php.

7. Cynthia Gorney. "The Changing Face of Saudi Women." *National Geographic.* 7 January 2016. http://ngm.nationalgeographic. com/2016/02/saudi arabia-women-text.

8. Ossob Mohamud, Ali Al-Ahmed. *Killing Them Softly.* Institute for Gulf Affairs, 2014. https://www.gulfinstitute.org/wp-content/ uploads/2014/12/Killing-Them-Softly.pdf.

9. "Labor Force Participation Rate, Female (% of Female Population Ages 15+)." *The World Bank.* 2015. http://data.worldbank.org/ indicator/SL.TLF.CACT.FE.ZS.

10. Abdullah Hamidaddin. "Hope for Female Unemployment In Saudi Arabia?" *Al Arabiya News.* 15 October 2015. Web. http://english.alarabiya.net/en/views/news/middle-east/2015/ 10/15/Hope-for-female-unemployment-in-Saudi-Arabia-.html.

11. Angus McDowall. "More Than 1 Million Saudis on Unemployment Benefit." *Reuters.* 28 March 2012. Web. http://www.reuters.com/ article/us-saudi-unemployment-subsidy-idUSBRE82R0L320120328.

12. David Miller. "Saudi Arabia Opens World's Largest Women's University." *The Jerusalem Post.* 17 May 2011. Web. http://www.jpost.com/Middle-East/Saudi-Arabia-opens- worlds-largest-womens-university.

13. Jacob Poushter. "How People in Muslim Countries Prefer Women to Dress in Public." Pew Research Center. 8 January 2014. http://www.pewresearch.org/fact-tank/2014/01/08/what-is- appropriate-attire-for-women-in-muslim-countries/.

14. "The Growing Role of Professional Women in Saudi Society." *Planet Arabia*. 2001. Web. http://www.mafhoum.com/press2/73S22.htm.

15. Anonymous for personal safety. Personal interview with Saudi woman. Washington, D.C., 18 February 2016.

16. "'Driving Affects Ovaries' . . . Saudi Fatwa Unleashes Wave of Mockery." *Middle East Online*. 29 September 2013. Web. http://www.middle-east-online.com/english/?id=61653.

17. Susie of Arabia, "On Gender Equality." http://susiesbigadventure.blogspot.com/2015/11/on-gender-equality.html.

18. Tariq A. Al Maeena. "A Fresh Perspective on Women Drivers." *Gulf News*. 1 December 2012. http://gulfnews.com/opinion/thinkers/a-fresh-perspective-on-women-drivers-1.1113004.

19. "Women's Right to Drive." *Saudi Women Driving*. 15 March 2016. http://saudiwomendriving.blogspot.com/.

20. Mohammed Jamjoom. "2 Saudi Women Detained for Driving in Ongoing Bid to End Ban." *CNN*. 3 December 2013. Web. http://www.cnn.com/2013/12/01/world/meast/saudi-arabia-female-drivers-detained/.

21. Fernande van Tets. "No woman, No drive." *The Independent*. 30 October 2013. http://www.independent.co.uk/arts-entertainment/music/news/no-woman-no-drive-song-about-saudi-arabia-s-ban-on-female-motorists-hits-right-note-on-youtube-8913822.html.

22. "'Sharing is Caring': Why Many Saudi Women Don't Mind Polygamy." *Al Arabiya News*. 27 September 2012. http://www.alarabiya.net/articles/2012/09/27/240384.html.

23. Afshan Aziz. "'Many Young People Oppose Polygamy.'" *Arab News*. 26 October 2015. http://www.arabnews.com/saudi-arabia/news/825906.

24. Habib Toumi. "Saudi Arabia Grand Mufti Says No Opposition to Underage Marriage." *Gulf News.* 21 December 2014. Web. http://gulfnews.com/news/gulf/saudi-arabia/saudi-arabia-grand-mufti-says-no-opposition-to-underage-marriage-1.1429882.

25. Kristine Beckerle. "Those Newly Elected Saudi Women Just Got Pushed Away from the Table." *Women's E-News.* 25 February 2016. http://womensenews.org/2016/02/those-newly-elected-saudi-women-just-got-pushed-away-from-the-table/.

26. Medea Benjamin. "Can an Election in Which Fewer Than 1 Percent of Eligible Saudi Women Voted Be Called a Victory?" *Salon.* 16 December 2015. Web. http://www.salon.com/2015/12/16/saudi_womens_vote_partner/.

27. Hala Aldosari. Personal Interview with Saudi scholar. Washington, D.C., 4 December 2015.

28. Lara Rebello. "900 Women Run for Office in Saudi Arabia's First Female-Inclusive Elections." *International Business Times.* 3 December 2015. http://www.ibtimes.co.uk/900-women-run-office-saudi-arabias-first-female-inclusive-elections-1531603.

29. Cynthia Gorney. "The Changing Face of Saudi Women." *National Geographic.* 7 January 2016. http://ngm.nationalgeographic.com/2016/02/saudi-arabia-women-text.

CHAPTER 5

1. Human Rights Watch. *World Report 2015: Saudi Arabia.* New York: Human Rights Watch, 2015. Web. https://www.hrw.org/world-report/2015/country-chapters/saudi-arabia.

2. Matthew J. Gibney and Randall Hansen. *Immigration and Asylum: From 1900 to the Present, 3 Volume Set.* Santa Barbara: ABC-CLIO, 2005. Print.

3. Graham Peebles. "The Abuse of Migrant Workers in Saudi
    Arabia." *Redress Information & Analysis.* 8 December 2013.
    Web. http://www.redressonline.com/2013/12/the-abuse-of-
    migrant-workers-in-saudi-arabia/.
4. "'As If I Am Not Human': Abuses Against Asian Domestic
    Workers in Saudi Arabia." *Human Rights Watch.* 7 July 2008. Web.
    https://www.hrw.org/report/2008/07/07/if-i-am-not-human/
    abuses-against-asian-domestic-workers-saudi-arabia.
5. "Detained, Beaten, Deported: Saudi Abuses Against
    Migrants During Mass Expulsions." *Human Rights Watch.*
    10 May 2015. Web. https://www.hrw.org/report/2015/05/10/
    detained-beaten-deported/saudi-abuses-against-migrants-
    during-mass-expulsions#page.
6. United States. Department of State. Office to Monitor and Combat
    Trafficking in Person. *2014 Trafficking in Persons Report.* 2014. Web.
    http://www.state.gov/j/tip/rls/tiprpt/countries/2014/226806
    .htm.
7. Rosie Bsheer. "Kafal Politics and Domestic Labor in
    Saudi Arabia." *Jadaliyya.* 17 September 2010. Web.
    http://www.jadaliyya.com/pages/index/153/kafala-
    politics-and-domestic-labor-in-saudi-arabia-.
8. Madawi al-Rasheed. "Maid in Saudi Arabia." *Almonitor.* 17 July
    2013. Web. http://www.al-monitor.com/pulse/fr/originals/2013/
    07/humantrafficking-saudiarabia-al-rasheed.html#.
9. "Saudi Arabia: Domestic Worker Brutalized." *Human Rights
    Watch.* 2 September 2010. Web. https://www.hrw.org/news/2010/
    09/02/saudi-arabia-domestic-worker-brutalized.
10. Khaled Al-Shaei. "Indonesians Outraged by Maids' Torture
    in Saudi Arabia." *Al Arabiya News.* 21 November 2010. Web.
    https://www.alarabiya.net/articles/2010/11/21/126841.html.

11. MediaMac. "Horrific Burns Suffered by Filipino Maid After Saudi Boss Threw Boiling Water at Her." Online video clip. *YouTube.* 21 May 2014. Web. https://www.youtube.com/watch?v=CZAIbxnK4cE.

12. "India Protests After Maid's Arm Cut Off in Saudi Arabia." *Aljazeera.* 9 October 2015. Web. http://www.aljazeera.com/news/2015/10/india-protests-maid-arm-cut-saudi-arabia-151009142232220.html.

13. Katy Migiro. "Desperate Kenyan Maids Abused in Middle East Despite Ban." *Reuters.* 26 May 2015. Web. http://www.reuters.com/article/us-rights-domesticworkers-kenya-idUSKBN0OC02K20150527.

14. Jason Burke. "Maid 'Held Hostage' for 14 Years in Saudi Arabia." *The Guardian.* 22 June 2011. Web. http://www.theguardian.com/world/2011/jun/22/maid-held-hostage-saudi-arabia.

15. Peebles, "The Abuse of Migrant Workers in Saudi Arabia." http://www.redressonline.com/2013/12/the-abuse-of-migrant-workers-in-saudi-arabia/.

16. "Prevent Abuses Against Migrant Domestic Workers." *Human Rights Watch.* 23 November 2010. Web. https://www.hrw.org/news/2010/11/23/prevent-abuses-against-migrant-domestic-workers.

17. Human Rights Watch, "Detained, Beaten, Deported." https://www.hrw.org/report/2015/05/10/detained-beaten-deported/saudi-abuses-against-migrants-during-mass-expulsions#page.

18. Human Rights Watch, "Saudi Arabia: Steps Toward Migrant Workers' Rights." https://www.hrw.org/news/2015/11/15/saudi-arabia-steps-toward-migrant-workers-rights.

19. Rashid Hassan. "'Beaten Up By Employer,' Indians to Return Home." *Arab News.* 25 December 2015. Web. http://www.arabnews.com/saudi-arabia/news/855516.

20. Sara Malm. "Saudi Husband Is Caught Groping and Forcing Himself on His Maid after His Suspicious Wife Set Up a Hidden Camera . . . But Now SHE Faces Going to Jail." *Daily Mail.* 7 October 2015. Web. http://www.dailymail.co.uk/news/article-3263250/Saudi-husband-caught-groping-forcing-maid-suspicious-wife-set-hidden-camera-faces-going-jail.html.

CHAPTER 6

1. Carol E.B. Choksy and Jamsheed K. Choksy. "The Saudi Connection: Wahhabism and Global Jihad." *World Affairs.* May 2015. http://www.worldaffairsjournal.org/article/saudi-connection-wahhabism-and-global-jihad.
2. Jeffrey Goldberg. "The Obama Doctrine." *The Atlantic.* April 2016. http://www.theatlantic.com/magazine/archive/2016/04/the-obama-doctrine/471525/.
3. Freedom House. *Saudi Arabia's Curriculum of Intolerance.* Washington, D.C.: Center for Religious Freedom, 2006. https://freedomhouse.org/sites/default/files/CurriculumOfIntolerance.pdf.
4. United States Commission on International Freedom. *USCIRF Annual Report 2014: Saudi Arabia.* 2014. http://www.uscirf.gov/sites/default/files/Saudi%20Arabia%202014.pdf.
5. Pierre Tristam. "1979 Seizure of the Grand Mosque in Mecca." *About News.* 25 November 2014. http://middleeast.about.com/od/terrorism/a/me081120b.htm.
6. Choksy and Choksy. "The Saudi Connection : Wahhabism and Global Jihad." http://www.worldaffairsjournal.org/article/saudi-connection-wahhabism-and-global-jihad.
7. Mark Mazzettif and Matt Apuzzo. "U.S. Relies Heavily on Saudi Money to Support Syrian Rebels." *The New York Times.* 23 January

2016. http://www.nytimes.com/2016/01/24/world/middleeast/us-relies-heavily-on-saudi-money-to-support-syrian-rebels.html?_r=0.

8. "Who are the Taliban?" *BBC News.* 29 September 2015. http://www.bbc.com/news/world-south-asia-11451718.

9. Patrick E. Tyler. "A Nation Challenged: The Family; Fearing Harm, Bin Laden Kin Fled from U.S." *The New York Times.* 30 September 2001. http://www.nytimes.com/2001/09/30/world/a-nation-challenged-the-family-fearing-harm-bin-laden-kin-fled-from-us.html.

10. United States Senate Select Committee on Intelligence and House Permanent Select Committee on Intelligence. *Joint Inquiry Into Intelligence Community Activities Before and After the Terrorist Attacks of September 11, 2001.* 107th Congress, 2nd Session. Washington, D.C.: 2002. https://fas.org/irp/congress/2002_rpt/911rept.pdf.

11. "Congressmen Reiterate Call for Release of 9/11 Secrets." *28pages.org.* 8 September 2015. http://28pages.org/2015/09/08/congressmen-reiterate-call-for-release-of-911-secrets/.

12. Brian McGlinchey. "MAJOR DEVELOPMENT: Rand Paul, Ron Wyden to Introduce 28 Pages Bill in Senate." *28Pages.org.* 28 May 2015. http://28pages.org/.

13. Carl Hulse. "Florida Ex-Senator Pursues Claims of Saudi Ties to Sept. 11 Attacks." *The New York Times.* 13 April 2015. http://www.nytimes.com/2015/04/14/world/middleeast/florida-ex-senator-pursues-claims-of-saudi-ties-to-sept-11-attacks.html.

14. Carl Hulse. "Claims Against Saudis Cast New Light on Secret Pages of 9/11 Report." *The New York Times.* 4 February 2015. http://www.nytimes.com/2015/02/05/us/claims-against-saudis-cast-new-light-on-secret-pages-of-9-11-report.html.

15. Karen Armstrong. "Wahhabism to ISIS: How Saudi Arabia Exported the Main Source of Global Terrorism." *New Statesman.* 27 November 2014. http://www.newstatesman.com/world-affairs/2014/11/wahhabism-isis-how-saudi-arabia-exported-main-source-global-terrorism.

16. Daniel Lazare. "How Saudi/Gulf Money Fuels Terror." *Consortium News.* 14 November 2015. https://consortiumnews.com/2015/11/14/how-saudigulf-money-fuels-terror/.

17. "US Embassy Cables: Hillary Clinton Says Saudi Arabia 'a Critical Source of Terrorist Funding.'" *The Guardian.* 30 December 2009. http://www.theguardian.com/world/us-embassy-cables-documents/242073.

18. Brian Fishman, et al. *Bombers, Bank Accounts, and Bleedout: Al-Qa'da's Road In and Out of Iraq.* CreateSpace Independent Publishing Platform, 2008. Print.

19. Barbara Wesel. "Brussels' Great Mosque and Ties with Salafism." *Deutsche Welle.* 21 November 2015. http://www.dw.com/en/brussels-great-mosque-and-ties-with-salafism/a-18866998.

20. Axel Schmidt. "German Vice Chancellor Warns Saudi Arabia over Islamist Funding." *Reuters.* 6 December 2015. http://www.reuters.com/article/us-saudi-germany-idUSKBN0TP0H720151206.

21. Christopher M. Blanchard. *Saudi Arabia: Background and U.S. Relations.* Congressional Research Service. 2016. https://www.fas.org/sgp/crs/mideast/RL33533.pdf.

22. The Soufan Group. *Foreign Fighters: An Updated Assessment of the Flow of Foreign Fighters into Syria and Iraq.* 2015. http://soufangroup.com/wp-content/uploads/2015/12/TSG_ForeignFightersUpdate3.pdf.

23. "92% of Saudis Believe That 'Islamic State Conforms to the Values of Islam and Islamic Law'—Poll." *Muslim Statistics.*

24 August 2014. https://muslimstatistics.wordpress.com/2014/08/24/92-of-saudis-believes-that-isis-conforms-to-the-values-of-islam-and-islamic-law-survey/.

24. Maria Khan. "US Vice President Joe Biden Apologises After Calling Sunni Allies 'Largest Problem in Syria.'" *International Business Times*. 5 October 2014. http://www.ibtimes.co.uk/us-vice-president-joe-biden-apologizes-after-calling-sunni-allies-largest-problem-syria-1468602.

25. Adam Taylor. "What Saudi Arabia Is (and Isn't) Doing in the Fight against ISIS." *The Boston Globe*. 25 November 2015. https://www.bostonglobe.com/news/world/2015/11/25/what-saudi-arabia-and-isn-doing-fight-against-isis/K8dauGJpUGOcSLbSuQ7QLM/story.html.

26. United States. US Department of State. Bureau of Counterterrorism. *Country Reports: Middle East and North Africa Overview*. 2013. http://www.state.gov/j/ct/rls/crt/2013/224823.htm.

27. Chris Zambelis. "To Topple the Throne: Islamic State Sets Its Sights on Saudi Arabia." The Jamestown Foundation. 6 March 2015. http://www.jamestown.org/programs/tm/single/?tx_ttnews[tt_news]=43625&cHash=9f42e030fa6e8e47a53701a4da6dee4d#.VvlBP3QrKHJ.

28. "Saudi Shura Member Spots 'Need' to Revise Terrorist Rehab Program." Al Arabiya News. 16 December 2016. http://english.alarabiya.net/en/News/middle-east/2014/12/16/Saudi-Shura-member-Need-to-revise-terrorist-rehabilitation-program.html.

29. "'ISIS is Enemy No. 1 of Islam,' Says Saudi Grand Mufti." *Al Arabiya News*. 19 August 2014.

30. "Fueling Terror." *Institute for the Analysis of Global Security*. 2004. http://english.alarabiya.net/en/News/middle-east/2014/08/19/Saudi-mufti-ISIS-is-enemy-No-1-of-Islam-.html.

31. Kamel Daoud. "Saudi Arabia, an ISIS That Has Made It." *The New York Times*. 20 November 2015. http://www.nytimes.com/2015/11/21/opinion/saudi-arabia-an-isis-that-has-made-it.html.

CHAPTER 7

1. "A DAY OF TERROR; Bush's Remarks to the Nation on the Terrorist Attacks." *The New York Times*. 12 September 2001. http://www.nytimes.com/2001/09/12/us/a-day-of-terror-bush-s-remarks-to-the-nation-on-the-terrorist-attacks.html.
2. Jeffrey Goldberg. "The Obama Doctrine." *The Atlantic*. April 2016. http://www.theatlantic.com/magazine/archive/2016/04/the-obama-doctrine/471525/.
3. Megan K. Stack. "King Abdullah, 90, of Saudi Arabia Dies; Obama Praises 'Candid' Leader." *The Los Angeles Times*. 22 January 2015. http://www.latimes.com/local/obituaries/la-me-king-abdullah-20150122-story.html.
4. United States. Department of State. Office of the Historian. *Foreign Relations of the United States 1955–1957 Volume XIII, Near East: Jordan-Yemen, Document 200*. 23 December 1955. https://history.state.gov/historicaldocuments/frus1955-57v13/d200.
5. "Militant Activity of Osama Bin Laden: Jihad in Afghanistan." *America Pink*. http://america.pink/militant-activity-osama-bin-laden_3015912.html.
6. "Osama Bin Laden v. the U.S.: Edicts and Statements." *PBS Frontline*. http://www.pbs.org/wgbh/pages/frontline/shows/binladen/who/edicts.html.
7. "Saudi Arabia—United States Relations." *Wikipedia*. 22 March 2016. https://en.wikipedia.org/wiki/Saudi_Arabia%E2%80%93United_States_relations.

MEDEA BENJAMIN

8. United States. The White House. Office of the Press Secretary. *Fact Sheet: United States–Saudi Arabia Bilateral Relationship.* https://www.whitehouse.gov/the-press-office/2014/03/28/fact-sheet-united-states-saudi-arabia-bilateral-relationship.

9. "Country Profile: Saudi Arabia." *Federation of American Scientists.* March 2002. http://fas.org/asmp/profiles/saudi_arabia.htm.

10. Khaled Abdullah. "Use of Cluster Bombs in Yemen May Be War Crime: U.N. Chief." *Reuters.* 8 January 2016. http://www.reuters.com/article/us-yemen-security-un-idUSKBN0UM23H20160108

11. Sarah Lazare. "Despite Atrocities, US Approves $1.29 Billion Deal to Re-Arm Saudi Arabia." *Common Dreams.* 17 November 2015. http://www.commondreams.org/news/2015/11/17/despite-atrocities-usapproves-129-billion-deal-re arin-saudi-arabia

12. "Press Release: President Obama Must Cancel $1.29b Arms Deal With Saudi Arabia." *Amnesty International.* 10 December 2015. http://www.amnesty usa.org/news/press-releases/presidentobama-must-cancel-129b-arms-deal-with-saudi-arabia

13. Mary Atkinson. "UK Could Freeze Arms Sales to Saudi Arabia Over Yemen Strikes." *Middle East Eye.* 11 November 2015. http://www.middleeasteye.net/news/uk-could-halt-arms-sales-saudi-arabiaover-yemen strikes-271051017

14. Nicholas Watt and Alan Travis. "UK Ditches Plan to Bid for 5.9£m Saudi Arabia Prisons Contract." *The Guardian.* 13 October 2015. http://www.theguardian.com/world/2015/oct/13/uk-ditches-plan-to-bid-for-saudi-arabia-prisons-contract.

15. Linda Åkerström. Personal interview. March 8 2016.

16. Robin Emmott. "European Parliament Calls for Saudi Arms Embargo." *Reuters.* 25 February 2016. http://www.reuters.com/article/us-eu-saudi-arms-idUSKCN0VY1K1.

17. Anthony Deutsch. "Dutch Parliament Votes to Ban Weapon Exports to Saudi Arabia." *Reuters.* 15 March 2016. http://uk.reuters .com/article/uk-netherlands-saudi-arms-idUKKCN0WH2T4.

18. "United States Military Training Mission: Home." *United States Military Training Mission: Riyadh, Saudi Arabia.* 1 November 2015. http://usmtm.org/.

19. Christopher M. Blanchard. *Saudi Arabia: Background and U.S. Relations.* Congressional Research Service, 2016. https://www .fas.org/sgp/crs/mideast/RL33533.pdf.

20. Mark Mazzetti, and Matt Apuzzo. "U.S. Relies Heavily on Saudi Money to Support Syrian Rebels." *The New York Times.* 23 January 2016. http://www.nytimes.com/2016/01/24/world/middleeast/ us-relies-heavily-on-saudi-money-to-support-syrian-rebels. html.

21. Mark Thompson. "A Question for the Obama Administration: Has the U.S. Wasted $8 Trillion Defending the Flow of Oil from the Persian Gulf?" *Time* magazine. 24 April 2011. http://nation .time.com/2011/04/24/a-question-for-the-obama-administration/.

22. Greg Fountain. "US-Gulf Defence Conference Plan." *Gulf Digital News.* 8 December 2013. http://archives.gdnonline.com/ NewsDetails.aspx?date=04/07/2015&storyid=366404.

23. Mark Hensch. "Trump: Saudi Arabia 'Should Pay Us.'" *The Hill.* 16 August 2015. http://thehill.com/blogs/ballot-box/ presidential-races/251227-trump-saudi-arabia-should-pay-us.

24. "Frequently Asked Questions: How Much Petroleum Does the United States Import and from Where." *U.S. Energy Information Administration.* 2015. http://www.eia.gov/tools/ faqs/faq.cfm?id=727&t=6.

25. Stephen Foley. "Revealed: Saudi Royals' Secret $1bn US Empire." *The Independent.* 6 June 2012. http://www.independent.co.uk/

news/business/news/revealed-saudi-royals-secret-1bn-us-empire-7817936.html.

26. United States. The White House. Office of the Press Secretary. *Fact Sheet: United States-Saudi Arabia Bilateral Relationship.* https://www.whitehouse.gov/the-press-office/2014/03/28/fact-sheet-united-states-sandi arabia-bilateral-relationship.

27. Lee Fang. "The Saudi Lobbying Complex Adds a New Member: GOP Super PAC Chair Norm Coleman." *The Nation.* 18 September 2014. http://www.thenation.com/article/saudi-lobbying-complex-adds-new-member-gop-super-pac-chair-norm-coleman/.

28. "Wash, DC PR Firm Accused of Whitewashing Work for Saudis." *Truth Revolt.* 21 March 2016. http://www.truthrevolt.org/news/wash-dc-pr-firm-accused-whitewashing-work-saudis.

29. Lee Fang. "Saudi Arabia Continues Hiring Spree of Lobbyists, Retains Former 'Washington Post' Reporter." *The Intercept.* 21 March 2016. https://theintercept.com/2016/03/21/saudi-arabia-continues-hiring-spree-of-lobbyists-retains-former-washington-post-reporter/.

30. Megan Wilson. "Saudis Have Lobbying Muscle for 9/11 Fight." *The Hill.* 18 April 2016. http://thehill.com/policy/international/276741-saudis-have-lobbying-muscle-for-9-11-fight.

31. Fang. "The Saudi Lobbying Complex Adds a New Member: GOP Super PAC Chair Norm Coleman." http://www.thenation.com/article/saudi-lobbying-complex-adds-new-member-gop-super-pac-chair-norm-coleman/.

32. Catherine Ho. "Saudi Government Has Vast Network of PR, Lobby Firms in the U.S." *The Washington Post.* 20 April 2016. https://www.washingtonpost.com/news/powerpost/wp/2016/04/20/saudi-government-has-vast-network-of-pr-lobby-firms-in-u-s/.

33. Max Fisher. "How Saudi Arabia Captured Washington." *Vox.* 21 March 2016. http://www.vox.com/2016/3/21/11275354/saudi-arabia-gulf-washington.

34. Richard Wike. "The World Gives Saudi Arabia Poor Marks on Freedoms." *Pew Research Center.* 28 March 2014. http://www.pewresearch.org/fact-tank/2014/03/28/the-world-gives-saudi-arabia-poor-marks-on-freedoms/.

35. David Pollock. "New Saudi Poll Shows Iran, Russia, United States, and ISIS Are All Unpopular; Mixed Views on Others." *The Washington Institute for Near East Policy.* 22 October 2015. http://www.washingtoninstitute.org/policy-analysis/view/new-saudi-poll-shows-iran-russia-united-states-and-isis-are-all-unpopular-m.

36. United States. Department of State. Bureau of Consular Affairs. "Saudi Arabia Travel Warning." 21 September 2015. http://travel.state.gov/content/passports/en/alertswarnings/saudi-arabia-travel-warning.html.

37. United States. The White House. Office of the Press Secretary. *Fact Sheet: United States–Saudi Arabia Bilateral Relationship.* https://www.whitehouse.gov/the-press-office/2014/03/28/fact-sheet-united-states-saudi-arabia-bilateral-relationship.

38. Stephen Kinzer. "Terrorism in Paris, Sydney the Legacy of Colonial Blunders." *The Boston Globe.* 18 January 2015. https://www.bostonglobe.com/opinion/2015/01/18/terrorism-paris-sydney-legacy-colonial-blunders/oEY5qPoluGRIZDC8UfNEyH/story.html.

39. "Frequently Asked Questions: How Much Petroleum Does the United States Import and from Where." *U.S. Energy Information Administration.* http://www.eia.gov/tools/faqs/faq.cfm?id=727&t=6.

CHAPTER 8

1. Military Expenditure Database. *Stockholm International Peace Research Institute.* November 2015. http://www.sipri.org/research/armaments/milex/milex_database/milex_database.

2. John R. Bradley. *Saudi Arabia Exposed: Inside a Kingdom in Crisis.* New York: Palgrave Macmillan and Houndmills, 2005.

3. Igor Pejic. "Military Analysis: Saudi Arabia's Armed Forces." *South Front.* 15 January 2016. https://southfront.org/military-analysis-saudi-arabia/.

4. Helene Cooper and Gardiner Harris. "An Arms Deal Is Aimed at Saudis' Iran Worries." *The New York Times.* 3 September 2015. http://www.nytimes.com/2015/09/04/us/politics/iran-deal-will-top-agenda-when-saudi-king-visits-white-house.html.

5. Jon Schwarz. "One Map That Explains the Dangerous Saudi-Iranian Conflict." *The Intercept.* 6 January 2016. https://theintercept.com/2016/01/06/one-map-that-explains-the-dangerous-saudi-iranian-conflict/.

6. Kelly McEvers. "Bahrain: The Revolution That Wasn't." NPR. 5 January 2012. http://www.npr.org/2012/01/05/144637499/bahrain-the-revolution-that-wasnt.

7. Vijay Prashad. "The Tragedy of Yemen Is Not a Marginal One." *The New Arab.* 10 February 2016. https://www.alaraby.co.uk/english/comment/2016/2/10/the-tragedy-of-yemen-is-not-a-marginal-one.

8. "The Arab Peace Initiative." *Al Jazeera.* 28 March 2010. http://www.aljazeera.com/focus/2009/01/200912764650608370.html.

9. *Saudi Gazette.* "Saudi Arabia Welcomes U.N. Report on Israeli Crimes in Gaza." *Al Arabiya English.* 30 June 2015. http://english.alarabiya.net/en/News/middle-east/2015/06/30/Saudi-Arabia-welcomes-U-N-report-on-Israeli-crimes-in-Gaza.html.

10. Murtaza Hussain. "Israel's Clandestine Alliance with Gulf Arab States Is Going Public." *The Intercept.* 5 June 2015. https://theintercept.com/2015/06/05/israel-gcc-alliance-shall-named/.

11. Salman Rafi. "US Concerned as Saudi Arabia, Israel Team Up against Common Foe Iran." *Asia Times.* 9 September 2015. http://atimes.com/2015/09/us-concerned-as-saudi-arabia-israel-move-closer-to-thwart-iran/.

12. Mehdi Hasan. "Mehdi Hasan Speaks to Abdallah al-Mouallimi." *Twitter.* 25 March 2016. https://twitter.com/mehdirhasan/status/713361161161408512?s=03.

CHAPTER 9

1. Maria Gallucci. "Oil Crisis: Can Saudi Arabia Break Its Addiction and Save the Economy from Plunging Crude Prices?" *International Business Times.* 13 January 2016. http://www.ibtimes.com/oil-crisis-can-saudi-arabia-break-its-addiction-save-economy-plunging-crude-prices-2262134.

2. International Monetary Fund, Middle East and Central Asia Department. *Regional Economic Outlook: Middle East and Central Asia.* Washington, D.C.: International Monetary Fund, 2015. http://www.imf.org/external/pubs/ft/reo/2015/mcd/eng/pdf/menap1015.pdf.

3. Antonia Juhasz. "Suicidal Tendencies: How Saudi Arabia Could Kill the COP21 Negotiations in Paris." *Newsweek.* 9 December 2015. http://www.newsweek.com/saudi-arabia-cop21-paris-climate-change-negotiations-402992.

4. "Migration of a Million Saudi Worries the Shura." *Huffington Post.* 21 February 2016. http://www.huffpostarabi.com/2016/02/21/story_n_9284088.html.

MEDEA BENJAMIN

5. Rori Donaghy. "Senior Saudi Royal Urges Leadership Change for Fear of Monarchy Collapse." *Middle East Eye.* 22 September 2015. http://www.middleeasteye.net/news/saudi-arabia-senior royal-urges-change-amid-fears-monarchy-collapse-1612130905.

6. Daisy Carrington. "Twitter Campaign Highlights Poverty in Saudi Arabia." *CNN.* 6 September 2013. http://www.cnn.com/2013/09/05/world/meast/twitter-campaign-highlights-poverty/.

7. Nahlah Ayed. "Why Saudi Arabia Is the World's Top YouTube Nation." *CBC News.* 1 April 2013. http://www.cbc.ca/news/world/nahlah-ayed-why-saudi-arabia-is-the world-s-top-youtube-nation-1.1359187.

8. MEMRI TV Videos. "Saudi Woman Defies Religious Police: It Is None of Your Business If I Wear Nail Polish." Video clip. YouTube. 24 May 2012. https://www.youtube.com/watch?v=OpUUOYRLW3k.

9. "Saudi Activists Who Are They and What Do They Want?" *New Internationalist Magazine.* March 2016. http://newint.org/features/2016/03/01/saudi-activists/.

10. Jeffrey Goldberg. "The Obama Doctrine." *The Atlantic.* March 2016. http://www.theatlantic.com/magazine/archive/2016/04/the-obama-doctrine/471525/.

INDEX

MEDEA BENJAMIN

MEDEA BENJAMIN

MEDEA BENJAMIN

MEDEA BENJAMIN

MEDEA BENJAMIN

O/R C

Cypherpunks
Freedom and the Future of the Internet
JULIAN ASSANGE with JACOB APPELBAUM, ANDY MÜLLER-MAGUHN, AND JÉRÉMIE ZIMMERMANN

When Google Met Wikileaks
JULIAN ASSANGE

Kingdom of the Unjust
Behind the U.S.–Saudi Connection
MEDEA BENJAMIN

A Narco History
How the US and Mexico Jointly Created the "Mexican Drug War"
CARMEN BOULLOSA AND MIKE WALLACE

Beautiful Trouble
A Toolbox for Revolution
ASSEMBLED BY ANDREW BOYD WITH DAVE OSWALD MITCHELL

Bowie
SIMON CRITCHLEY

Extinction
A Radical History
ASHLEY DAWSON

Black Ops Advertising
Native Ads, Content Marketing, and the Covert World of the Digital Sell
MARA EINSTEIN

Beautiful Solutions
A Toolbox for Liberation
EDITED BY ELI FEGHALI, RACHEL PLATTUS, AND ELANDRIA WILLIAMS

Remembering Akbar
Inside the Iranian Revolution
BEHROOZ GHAMARI

Folding the Red into the Black
or Developing a Viable *Un*topia for Human Survival in the 21st Century
WALTER MOSLEY

Inferno
(A Poet's Novel)
EILEEN MYLES